Notorious Murders
of the
Twentieth Century

TRUE CRIME FROM WHARNCLIFFE
Foul Deeds and Suspicious Deaths Series

Barking, Dagenham & Chadwell Heath
Barnet, Finchley and Hendon
Barnsley
Bath
Bedford
Birmingham
Black Country
Blackburn and Hyndburn
Bolton
Bradford
Brighton
Bristol
Cambridge
Carlisle
Chesterfield
Colchester
Cotswolds, The
Coventry
Croydon
Derby
Dublin
Durham
Ealing
Fens, In and Around
Folkstone and Dover
Grimsby
Guernsey
Guildford
Halifax
Hampstead, Holborn and St Pancras
Huddersfield
Hull

Jersey
Leeds
Leicester
Lewisham and Deptford
Liverpool
London's East End
London's West End
Manchester
Mansfield
More Foul Deeds Birmingham
More Foul Deeds Chesterfield
More Foul Deeds Wakefield
Newcastle
Newport
Norfolk
Northampton
Nottingham
Oxfordshire
Pontefract and Castleford
Portsmouth
Rotherham
Scunthorpe
Shrewsbury and Around Shropshire
Southampton
Southend-on-Sea
Staffordshire and The Potteries
Stratford and South Warwickshire
Tees
Uxbridge
Warwickshire
Wigan
York

OTHER TRUE CRIME BOOKS FROM WHARNCLIFFE

A-Z of London Murders, The
A-Z of Yorkshire Murders, The
Black Barnsley
Brighton Crime and Vice 1800-2000
Crafty Crooks and Conmen
Durham Executions
Essex Murders
Executions & Hangings in Newcastle
  and Morpeth
Great Hoaxers, Artful Fakers and
  Cheating Charlatans
Norfolk Mayhem and Murder

Norwich Murders
Plot to Kill Lloyd George
Romford Outrage
Strangeways Hanged
Unsolved Murders in Victorian &
  Edwardian London
Unsolved London Murders
Unsolved Norfolk Murders
Unsolved Yorkshire Murders
Warwickshire's Murderous Women
Yorkshire Hangmen
Yorkshire's Murderous Women

Please contact us via any of the methods below for more information or a catalogue
WHARNCLIFFE BOOKS
47 Church Street, Barnsley, South Yorkshire, S70 2AS
Tel: 01226 734555 • 734222 • Fax: 01226 734438
email: enquiries@pen-and-sword.co.uk
website: www.wharncliffebooks.co.uk

Notorious Murders of the Twentieth Century

Famous and Forgotten British Cases

STEPHEN WADE

True Crime

First published in Great Britain in 2011 by
Wharncliffe Books
an imprint of
Pen and Sword Books Ltd
47 Church Street
Barnsley
South Yorkshire
S70 2AS

© Stephen Wade 2011

ISBN: 978-1-84563-130-7

The right of Stephen Wade to be identified as the author
of this work has been asserted by him in accordance with
the Copyright, Designs and Patents Act 1988.

A CIP catalogue record for this book is available from the
British Library.

Typeset in 11/13pt Plantin by Concept, Huddersfield.

Printed and bound in England by CPI UK.

Pen & Sword Books Ltd incorporates the imprints of
Pen & Sword Aviation, Pen & Sword Maritime,
Pen & Sword Military, Wharncliffe Local History,
Pen & Sword Select, Pen & Sword Military Classics,
Leo Cooper, Remember When, Seaforth Publishing and
Frontline Publishing.

For a complete list of Pen & Sword titles please contact
PEN & SWORD BOOKS LIMITED
47 Church Street
Barnsley
South Yorkshire
S70 2BR
England
E-mail: enquiries@pen-and-sword.co.uk
Website: www.pen-and-sword.co.uk

Contents

Introduction

Unfortunately, the crime of murder is extremely common, so much so that the majority of murders happen within relationships or are committed by people who know their victims. The 'famous' murders are the ones that are forever being written about – mainly by serial and mass killers. Every daily paper carries murder stories, and they tend to cause a stir, but that is no more than a wave rippling on an ocean. For a crime to really whip up a tempest there has to be an extraordinary element of evil, often with a psychological element. The really famous murders tend to have the adjective changed to 'infamous' and they are a subject of constant fascination. We may theorise endlessly about why a serial killer did what he or she did but in the end, there will be something enigmatic about it.

On the other hand, there have been a number of extraordinary murders which were undoubtedly famous and have remained so, albeit in the media that caters for true crime enthusiasts. Some are unsolved, and so they have their own mystery, others are simply strange and intriguing. They are forgotten in the sense of being out of the public eye, but there they still lie, in books, magazine articles and on the internet. Such are the subjects of this book.

Most murder cases also tend to follow a template which stems from the classic structure from the days of hanging, of:

(1) the crime;
(2) the pursuit;
(3) the arrest;
(4) the trial; and
(5) the closure – noose or cell.

Since 1964 this established courtroom drama, in which a trial really was a matter of life and death, has gone, although (as my last chapter shows) there were death sentences meted out from the Tynwald on the Isle of Man in the 1990s. Still, the really compelling famous murders tend to be either the unsolved or the highly sensational. For that reason, I wanted the cases re-told here to be either unfamiliar or classically mysterious. The mix selected is composed of four categories:

1. The classic unsolved – such as the Wallace case, in which several logistical problems related to Wallace's behaviour remain open.
2. The outright savage and brutal – perhaps best repre-sented by Buck Ruxton, whose case was also a forensic first.
3. The issue of a reprieve being given.
4. The bizarre and unexpected in a courtroom triumph – the clearest case here being that of Jeannie Donald.

Of course there are many other categories, such as a miscarriage of justice and indeed the most dramatic of all, a reprieve of a condemned woman, in the story of Florence Maybrick.

What persists, in the history of true crime writing, is the fascination of a voyeuristic perspective: the general reader, a lay person outside the professional arena of the detective, the judge or the pathologist, feels the most intense curiosity at the thought of what consequences may follow the taking of a human life. If that murder is by a husband, wife, son or daughter, then the voyeurism takes on another dimension: because most of us know family life and we know the stresses and demands of relationships, we therefore feel a certain level of insight and empathy in these case; and this is nothing to do with the old adage that 'any one of us could take a life, if pushed too far'. That statement is always open to debate and it is far too simplistic.

What is murder?

In 1957, when the possible abolition of the death penalty for murder was in the air, an official report listed fifty homicides in Britain in the year preceding the publication of the paper. The authors noted that all fifty involved a factor which was either accidental or circumstantial: in other words, a killing with a possibility of manslaughter rather than murder. That simple difference is crucial, of course. In a murder, there have to be these two elements:

Mens rea – a guilty mind or intent (malice aforethought).
Actus reus – the elements of an offence excluding those which concern the mind of the accused.

There has to be an intent to take life or to act in such a way that death would be a possible outcome; then there has to be such an act taken.

An accepted definition of murder is: '. . . unlawful homicide committed with malice aforethought, express or implied. *Express malice* exists where the person killing does so with the intention of causing death or grievous bodily harm. *Implied malice* exists where the person killing does not actually intend to kill or do grievous bodily harm, yet intentionally does an act which to his knowledge is likely to cause death . . .' (*Mozley and Whiteley's Law Dictionary*)

There is also in the classic definition the added clause: '. . . the death occurring within a year and a day' and that has given a number of fascinating cases over the years in which the accused waits to see if the charge might be manslaughter or murder – the noose or a long spell inside. Also, in Britain, we have the issue of the *crime passionel*, and as Sir Harold Scott wrote as a commentary on this: 'Thus *crimes passionels* arising out of sexual jealousy amount to murder unless the jury considers that the provocation was enough to make a reasonable man do as the killer did through loss of self-control because of what he saw or of what was said to him.'

In popular culture, though, such fine distinctions hardly matter. The fact is that in a narrative in popular genres, a killer is a killer, and the ambivalence is of little interest. What always attract attention are the motives. A true crime murder story, like all stories, is about the question why. There are so many possible reasons for taking a life that every murder story will probably have a factor that is indicative of intentions that may or may not be provable as aims to kill. In other words, the commonest defence of 'I didn't mean to kill him/her' is hard to prove and also hard to disprove. Even more interesting is the killing done for money, a hit killing. There, there is an element of it being a 'business' and so motivations are plain and one-sided. There may well be other emotions beneath the surface but what arises in the heart of the story is killing for cash.

Of course, there are also 'firsts' and I start with the once famous case of the murders which were solved by means of fingerprints, and for which the fingerprint evidence was judged to be admissible. There were plenty of others in that category to choose from, but few forensics firsts have such appeal.

What about weapons and methods? The *modus operandi* in the majority of cases is plain and direct – poison, the blunt instrument, the blade or the bullet. Poisonings have always been prominent in the famous cases, and many of these are baffling in their complexity. But there are the straightforward approaches such as the Hay case when food was poisoned, and in fact consumed in the presence of the apparently amiable and well-respected killer. Poison is in some ways the expert's chosen means: this is because there is a wide choice, each with a different method of extinguishing life. There is a huge difference between the killer wanting the victim to die mercifully quickly, as with strychnine, and the poison which will provide a long and agonising death, as has often been the case with arsenic, given in small doses. The latter was complicated in Victorian times because, as with James Maybrick, arsenic was used in tiny doses as an aphrodisiac.

There are great murder stories too, in the sense that something about them captures the public imagination, and there is a strange element to this: something that creates almost a fictional feel to the tale. Of course that is because such affairs are distant from the man in the street and that distance lends an unreal quality. In my cases, the story of Guenther Podola perhaps comes closest to this. I was eleven when Podola shot a policeman dead – Sergeant Purdy. This was reported on television, and as it was 1959, it was the early days of television being in ordinary homes. I have a lingering image of a phone box being involved in the story and of the uproar at the thought of someone killing a police officer. The image was correct, as it turned out that Podola had rung his intended victim from a phone box at South Kensington underground station. What this illustrates is the tendency for prominent murder stories to haunt the imagination, just as a scene from a novel or a film might do.

I have three stories of police killings here, and that makes sense when we consider how much the officers are in the front line, taking the bullets as well as the threats. They often live in very dangerous situations, and their heroism in facing a gun barrel has figured in hundreds of famous murders – unfortunately many of which are forgotten. That is in the sense that they are a furore, but a temporary one until the next, more horrendous killing comes along. Crime magazines tend to make lists and write from the basis of the arithmetic of death: they make copy from questions about which serial killer has done the most murders, or who has committed the most disgusting killings.

It is significant though, that as I write this, there are eighteen criminals serving life sentences without the possibility of parole who were once infamous as well as famous and who are now in all the books about murder in Britain, yet the younger generation will not know them. The man who was once a horrific and highly dangerous killer is now a zombie on drugs, harmless and aged, walking a hospital ward or watching television and sipping cocoa, safely behind a very high wall. A murder story offers the most transient fame, and yet many lust after that 'cred' and what it brings both in jail and inside the covers of true crime books. Any accidental discovery of an old yellowing newspaper will confirm that. There will almost certainly be a headline asking who killed someone or quoting the numbers of the slain.

Why write about the famous but forgotten cases then? We write about such murders because they teach us, with very special insights, about the nature of the worst transgression, one of the key Ten Commandments, an act going back to Cain and Abel. They involve intricate questions of morality and they show that morality becomes entangled with the condition of the criminal law at the time of the events. At one point in time, the moral fabric of the community will be outraged by something that, some years later, is very ordinary. The obvious example is what is known in the slang of everyday talk as 'queer bashing'. In the days of Quentin Crisp and his adventures around London clubs, when gay men were targets for cruelty and violence, there were murders; and they illustrate the nature of the social context that existed before the acceptance of homosexuality within mainstream culture.

Another vivid example of this crossing of morality and law in murder cases is the murder trial involving a woman in the dock.

One of the most celebrated cases in Scottish history, that of Jeannie Donald (see Chapter 3), was something that reached out into a specific community, its geography, its patterns of behaviour and its integration and divisions. In other words, a murder can shine the torch of knowledge into the dark corners we previous ignored or chose to forget.

There is a literary tradition to crime writing about famous murders which tends to create a line of thinkers, each adding to what has gone before, and each developing a new theory. In my collection there is one outstanding example: that of William Herbert Wallace. As Douglas Wynn wrote in his book, *On Trial for Murder* (1996), 'This was one of the strangest murder cases ever. The murder reads like a detective story and there have been some twenty books written about it. Raymond Chandler called it the "impossible murder" ...' In writing my contribution to the debate, I am conscious that this murder case has gone so far into the realms of literature rather than life that I feel the creative weight of previous minds at work on the enigma.

Finally, as well as writing about killers, I have worked with several in the capacity of a writer working in prisons. The majority of murderers are sad individuals who made a bad choice of behaviour, lost control in a confrontation, or allowed something dark to enter the soul, something that took away the restraint, the block to action. A cold killer has no block, no filter to allow the right human feelings in at the crucial moment. The killers I have met have been people who would be horrified at the thought that some would think them 'evil'. A few I have worked with might perhaps relish the thought of that word being applied to them.

We now have a great deal of scientific knowledge applied to human aggression and the neuroscientists have developed theories about which parts of the brain may be damaged or tend to malfunction when it comes to applying violence. Whatever the causes, the killers in most cases, if we avoid ideological and religious elements, tend to slip into one of these three categories:

(1) The killer who is temporarily controlled by some urge that dominates the natural restraint we have from socialised behaviour.

(2) The killer who purposely allows the urge to take life into his or her being, for 'kicks' or for gain.
(3) The killer who places no value on human life and who sees murder merely as a business, a way of life.

Murder and memory make an interesting enquiry in this context. Ever since the street ballad singers and sellers of chapbooks sold a tale of 'a good murder' back in the Victorian period, the theme has been one of 'out of sight, out of mind'. Crowds of thousands swarmed to watch the hanging of Courvoisier, the man who murdered his aristocratic employer in 1840, but that was soon forgotten when the next hanging came along soon after. The subject causes sensations but they are fleeting ones, merely passing interests. But choosing which ones provide truly fascinating revisits from a crime writer has been full of interest, and in the end, the main attraction has been that of tantalising questions.

Choice has been immense: the same problem confronted Jonathan Goodman when he edited *The Daily Telegraph Murder File* volume. In his preface he says, 'When I came to choose according to the *Telegraph* accounts of matters to do with murder for this book, the Palmer case was already chosen. Deciding what else to include was made hardly less daunting by my having decided to stay within the 113 years till the abolition of capital punishment in Great Britain. During those years [since the founding of the *Telegraph*] there were some 40,000 known murders in England and Wales ...'

Writing about the crime of murder attracted its first grandly literary treatment in the hands of the writer who moved in the Wordsworth circle, Thomas de Quincey, and he more than anyone understood its appeal to readers other than those who hanker after tales of the noose and back-street garottings. He said, in his famous essay, *Murder Considered as One of the Fine Arts*, 'Murder may be laid hold of by its moral handle ... or it may be also treated aesthetically. As the Germans call it, that is, in relation to good taste ...' He was hinting at the way in which readers of crime stories tend to divide into those who see a murder as totally serious business, related to the close study of criminology, and those who enjoy the story on a more playful level, with little to do with the dark reality of its occasion.

Gershon Legman once wrote that 'Murder is a crime. Writing about it is not.' He was noting that there is an element of the subject which relates to the way we divorce the actual facts from the relish of the drama and sensation. This, after all, is there in the so-called 'cosy' genre of crime fiction, in contrast to the direct shock of a serial killer story or explicit forensic writing.

I have attempted to include both aspects of crime writing here – there is plenty of commentary on the harsh reality of someone taking a life, but also a dash of the aesthetic, as De Quincey would say.

Technology

Writing in 2004, Danny McGannan recalled working in computers early in his career:'As a computer operator in the 1970s, many frustrating night shifts were spent chasing a fast unwinding reel of paper tape containing criminal record details that had inexplicably made a bid for freedom from the noisy reader device. Tracking criminals took on a different meaning in those days.' The Police National Computer was established in 1974. Before then computer rooms were massive, taking up long and broad floors in huge buildings. It is common knowledge that, in the Yorkshire Ripper investigation, record-keeping and technological back-up were still in the pre-computer days, well before DNA and before the Phoenix Names Application which was introduced in 1995.

The Phoenix Application was the first step in the national database of names and historical information on convicted criminals. Since then there has been a second technological revolution. In 2005, for instance, an international police partnership was set up when the police computer was linked to the Schengen Information System which was created to integrate criminal information across Europe.

Today, DNA sampling is so sophisticated that we might think that it is becoming more difficult than ever to commit a murder and not be traced. In one sense that is so, yet there are over 1,000 unsolved murder cases in the United Kingdom. As a report given by BBC News in March 2010 stated, 'Detectives never close the files of unsolved homicides. They simply keep hoping that one day they will find the killer.' The BBC did a survey to find where the unsolved cases were; the Metropolitan Police, predictably, had 341, but the figures only go back as far as 1996. The West Midlands had 78 unsolved cases, Greater Manchester had 54 (for the last decade only) and Strathclyde had 53.

The following cases include one of the most annotated and investigated cold cases of them all in the regions: that of Christopher Laverack in Hull. The local studies library in the city (now part of the Hull History Centre) had several drawers of press cuttings; mention the case in Hull and the chances are that the listener will have an opinion.

Technology still only works when the right kind of police thinking is applied. Will O'Reilly retired recently from the Met and he told the press what happens in classic murder investigation thinking: 'Time is of the essence at the beginning of any investigation ... we talk about a golden hour where there is an opportunity to make progress – but that can often be pushed further to the first twenty-four hours and then the first forty-eight. But once you give up the crime scene, you start to lose things.' Current practice is for a murder to be considered cold when a team of detectives have met and agreed to box the papers; but paperwork is reviewed every two years.

The new forensic technology will improve matters, and continue to do so, but we can see from this how a case becomes 'cold'. Famous but forgotten cases are either constantly fascinating because we know all salient facts or because we know practically nothing. We know a great deal about the Wallace case but we do not know the killer.

CHAPTER 1

The First Fingerprint Conviction

*The advantage of fingerprints as a
means of proving identity is no longer
open to discussion ...*

Home Office Committee report (1900)

A lawyer as well as a writer, J P Eddy, noted in his 1960 autobiography: 'It was as a young journalist in London that I was brought into direct contact in 1905 with the first murder case in England in which fingerprint evidence was used.' He even added: 'I remember very well as a young journalist going to see the scene of the crime before writing an account of it.' But amazingly, he does not include that response in his memoirs. He was present at a truly significant event in criminal and legal history.

One of the most celebrated detectives of the twentieth century, Fred Cherrill ('Cherrill of the Yard'), explained his early fascination with fingerprints by telling the tale of his going to an old mill with his father in a storm. The miller was ill and someone was needed to grind the corn to meet demand. In the mill, flour was sprayed everywhere, putting a white film over every surface, and young Fred found himself grabbing an eel his father threw across the room at him, with orders to put it in a sack. His hands were caked in eel slime and then he writes, 'Startled, I put out a hand to steady myself. For just a moment my slime-covered fingers rested on the wooden chute, which had become highly polished by all the flour and meal which had passed over its surface ... I was gazing at the chute in awed fascination ... There, by the agency of nature alone, were my fingerprints!'

Cherrill's story accounts for the long history of the knowledge of fingerprints, long before they were used in forensics.

There had been various academics who had done work on prints but nothing had come of it: a professor at the University of Breslau in 1823 had read a Latin thesis on fingerprints in a lecture, and the artist Thomas Bewick had done some wood engravings of fingerprints, using them as identifying signatures on his works. In China, for many centuries, thumb-prints had been used in documents for identity purposes in ratification. Similarly, these impressions had been used in India with illiterate members of the population. When the scientist Francis Galton got to work on the subject, he wrote a book-length study, simply called *Fingerprints*, published in 1892. In some ways, the introduction of fingerprinting into police work is similar to the rivalry to reach the South Pole: while Sir Edward Henry was using fingerprints in India for crime investigation, the same work was being done in Argentina by Francesca Rojas. But after Henry had introduced fingerprinting into the repertoire of detection methods at the Yard, it was to effect a revolution in detective procedure.

The prototype scenario and first conviction by the use of prints came in 1902, when the Yard had around 100 finger-prints in their first small volume of records. It was a murder case, and it took place at Chapman's Oil and Colour Stores in Deptford. An old couple, Thomas and Ann Farrow, ran the shop and they had an assistant, young William Jones, who, along with Louis Kidman, found Thomas's corpse and later the still breathing Ann Farrow.

The old man had been brutally beaten, with a broken cheek-bone and a fractured skull. The doctor said that the man had died around ninety minutes earlier. When Ann Farrow had been taken to hospital and the scene was ready for some inspection, Chief Inspector Fred Fox arrived to do his work, with two photographers. Crime scene investigation, in something close to the modern sense, was being born that day. No less a figure than Melville Macnaghten came to assist and then took charge. The killer had not forced an entry, that was the first important detail established. There had been a frenzied search of the whole shop and house, but after going upstairs and hitting Mrs Farrow, the scene suggested that they had come downstairs and then fought the old man again, as he had recovered from their first blow.

There were no witnesses; three masks were found abandoned in the shop so now Macnaghten knew he was looking for three killers, and that made the murder all the more savage and reprehensible. There was no indication as to what weapon had been used in the murderous attacks either. The question now on the detective's mind was whether Ann Farrow would recover and give descriptions. What was particularly unhelpful in the course of following the usual tracing procedure in pawn shops and similar outlets, was that the killers had only taken money. That created a dead end in the normal line of enquiry. It was looking desperate for the Chief; another shopkeeper had been killed in London the same day. Then, the final blow, Mrs Farrow died.

Macnaghten went back to the bloodbath that was the sitting room of the Farrow household. Casting his eye across the room and the pools of blood, he thought of the surface prints that had just been perused in smaller scale arrests. Would the Farrow murder be the first opportunity to try this new device? He established that none of the police personnel at the shop had touched the cashbox, then he covered his fingers with a handkerchief and showed his team the print on the box. Collins, of the new Fingerprint Branch, was a sleuth with a scientific bent; he had been working on other types of basic forensics and was excited about this new technique. It was a matter of magnifying glasses and intense study at that time; he had a small collection of filed prints from known criminals and that was that. There had been a long-established method of filing basic records of habitual offenders, so there was some hope of a 'result'. But the print on the cash box had no match in Collins's shelves.

Only a month before this case, Collins had been called in to help define a prisoner's identity. This was the case of Albert Wilkinson, charged with theft and grievous bodily harm. He had been arrested on suspicion but his identity could not be proved. Police thought he was the same man who had committed a similar offence in Hull and elsewhere. Collins was called in and as there was a fingerprint on a document in the hands of the accused, a comparison was made. Collins, it was reported, '. . . compared the original impressions with those taken at Dartmoor of a convict named Hargreaves, who was sentenced at Hull for larceny . . . they were absolutely identical'. The Wilkinson case was surely in the minds of the legal professionals in court for or against the Strattons, and Collins was bristling with professional pride after that triumph.

Basic police work, however, provided the lead that would eventually take the investigation back to the cash box. A milkman at work on the day of the killing had seen two men leaving the shop and he gave a description of them. The milkman saw that they had left the door open and told them so but they took no notice as they said there was someone behind them. To tally with this, three men had been seen in a local pub very early that day – and they answered the descriptions. It was when a certain Ellen Stanton came forward that things accelerated; she had seen two men running at the right time, and they had the same appearance as two suspects, and Ellen knew one of them. Macnaghten was now searching for Alfred Stratton. The man was taken in Deptford. The identification parade failed, but Collins took the prints of Stratton and his brother. One print matched that of Alfred.

Other results from basic investigation had been productive, such as the evidence of a landlady that she had found a pair of silk stockings, which had been cut in such a way as to make masks, lying under the bed of Albert Stratton. These had been left at the paint shop.

What happened then is a pattern for almost all succeeding scientific forensic advances when it came to actually implementing the knowledge and seeing it take part in a process of law in the courts. In other words, this new detective force, with its fingerprints and other types of records, was going to find it hard to convince judge and jury about the new methods of detection. But the Stratton brothers went to the gallows; hangman John Billington officiated at Wandsworth. The judge, Mr Justice Channell, had said in court that the men should not be convicted on fingerprint evidence alone and that was the case. But the first trial involving fingerprint evidence had happened; from that point on the concept would be a little more familiar, and the newspapers played their part in ensuring that would be the case.

The court room drama was at the Old Bailey. Mr Justice Channell presided, and he and the jury was startled and surely impressed by Inspector Collins, who took an impression of a thumb from one of the members of the jury who had requested it. Collins demonstrated the difference in the whorls and lines with regard to the amount of pressure applied when the thumb was used.

Expert witnesses then clashed. The defence had brought in J G Garson, a man who had formerly been working for the Home Office and he spoke about the differences between Stratton's print and that on the cash box. He said that it was not impossible that these came from the same person, but in his professional opinion, they were from different hands. Was Stratton going to be saved from the scaffold? The answer lay in the hands of R D Muir for the prosecution, who used two letters written by the defence expert. It was to cast doubt on everything he had said. One letter was for the defence, claiming that the use of the fingerprints by the police was not sound and would ruin their reputation in that branch of forensics; but the other letter was to the Director of Public Prosecutions asking whether witnesses were to be called to give scientific interpretation. He wrote:

> I feel that the Government have perhaps the first claim on my services. I may say that if I am not retained by the Treasury as an expert I shall probably give evidence as such for the defence, and that is the reason I am desirous of knowing as soon as possible whether my services are required by the Treasury.

It would be useful to know where Muir obtained that letter, but the outcome was, naturally, devastating for the defence case. Muir asked the man, 'How can you reconcile the writing of those two letters on the same day?'

'I am an independent witness,' he replied.

'An absolutely untrustworthy one, I should think. After writing two such letters.'

Garson later wrote to *The Times* to defend his position and indeed his professional standing, saying, 'My intention was entirely on public grounds, and I hoped to place before the Crown the result of a careful independent examination of the fingerprints. It was in this sense, and in this sense only, that I offered to give evidence for the prosecution. Failing my being asked to place my statements before the Crown, I felt it a public duty to offer the same thing to the defence.' His argument had no effect and changed nothing with regard to public opinion.

J P Eddy explained the judge's summing up: '. . . he said that if it was correct that people's hands and fingers varied so much, there was at any rate an extraordinary amount of resemblance between the two marks and therefore to a certain extent it was corroborative evidence in regard to Alfred, though he did not think the jury would act on it alone.'

The brothers were found guilty. The judge had felt a certain reluctance to take the scientific evidence. His reservation was that 'the fingerprint system is used for the purpose of identifying a criminal who has been convicted once, and has been convicted again, in each of which cases a proper impression has been taken for the purpose, but it is a different thing to apply it to a casual mark made through the perspiration of a thumb'.

He had not grasped the significance of the new weapon in the forensic armoury. As Fred Cherrill commented on the case: 'Unfortunately murderers do not walk about with bottles of ink, and we have to work with what we find. But that does not make our conclusions any the less certain.'

As for Alfred and Albert Stratton, they were hanged on 23 May that year at Wandsworth, by John Billington, with Henry Pierrepoint and John Ellis assisting.

What was happening in the closing years of the nineteenth century and the first years of the new century was that Scotland Yard was acquiring a much more sophisticated records department than ever before and fingerprints were beginning to play a major part in that. Edward Henry initiated the Central Fingerprint Bureau and together with the Register of Habitual Criminals, the Criminal Records Office was created. Three CID men, Stedman, Collins and Hunt, were to run the new section.

Fred Cherrill's memoirs give us an insight into what the Fingerprint Bureau was like in its early days; he joined it in 1920, when it was in the old part of Scotland Yard. Cherrill was working, in his early years, with the same format of records that had existed fifteen years before: these were various anthropometric sources and he was very critical of this 'chest of drawers':

'The intrinsic value was nil. But to me it had more than a little sentimental appeal.' It was, in fact, the basic product of the system begun by Alphonse Bertillon (1853–1914) who had been a worker in the Paris Prefecture of Police records department. *Bertillonage* became the method of classification by 'mugshot' as he had been interested in using photography for recording purposes. His *portrait parle* became a standard concept in visual records of criminals. He was opposed to fingerprinting and thought that photographs were the better means of identification. He had worked out that the chances of two people of similar profiles being exactly the same height were four to one. He extended this to all areas of dimensions in all parts of the frame and so produced a template for individualising the subject. If the subject were to be a criminal, then think of the value of that in the detective's records.

The Deptford case, known generally as The Mask Murder, is undoubtedly famous for many reasons, but most clearly for the credibility and admissibility in law of fingerprints – something now completely matter of fact and accepted without question.

In 1953, the report from the Commissioner of Police of the Metropolis was presented to Parliament and in that report it was stated that the fingerprint collection at Scotland Yard at that time was over 500,000 prints. Between the Stratton case and the date of that report – covering fifty years of police history – there was only one other fingerprint issue at the court of appeal: one in which a burglar claimed that his prints found on a candle could have been put there by one of his gang. The appeal failed, and Lord Darling's question was the only one that ever carried the day. He asked, 'Can the prisoner find anybody whose fingerprints are exactly like his?' That simple question reflects a massive revolution in forensics.

CHAPTER 2

Poison in Idyllic Hay-on-Wye

Armstrong was hen-pecked and
his wife made no secret of the fact
that she ruled him.

Robert Jackson

In my childhood in the 1950s, an everyday sight was the number of dangling brownish strips of paper hanging from the ceiling, usually by the light: these were fly-papers, and they were loaded with arsenic. Even at that time, arsenic had such domestic uses. It was still, in spite of various controlling acts, a familiar domestic poison. It had also been a substance with a very long history of use as a method of murder, and this story is one of the most celebrated cases of that horrific means of taking life.

Hay-on-Wye, Brecon, is Wales' 'town of books'. Today, it is a place with a prestigious literary festival and flocks of book-loving visitors, principally in the summer months. People wander and browse in the dust-caked shelves of old books, chat and eat ice-creams, sip soft drinks and stare into the peaceful vista towards Hereford. Even more idyllic is the hamlet of Cusop Dingle just half a mile down the road, and there lived a killer, a man with murderous designs on his wife and on a fellow lawyer. This prosperous, amiable man's spirit haunts that tranquil place. A moment's reflection will bring to mind a former Hay, a place where farmers met and where the vicar and diarist Francis Kilvert would walk and meet the ordinary folk who respected him, just as they respected Major Armstrong, clerk to the magistrates and local solicitor – and poisoner, with a penchant for applying arsenic to scones.

The case of Major Armstrong and the poisoning of his wife in the quiet market town of Hay-on-Wye is one which has been written about almost in the melodramatic manner of the

television series, *Midsummer Murders*. The reason for this is that
the ingredients of the tale are highly dramatic and are also
riddled with clichés and standard 'characters'. The Major himself was a natty dresser and charming company, diminutive and
chirpy, well liked in the community. His wife was domineering
and from a good family. He was a Cambridge man but was by
no means upper class in his origins. To cap all this, we have in
the Hay poisoning case the established storyline of professional
rivalry and ambition, with ironic twists all along the way. Yet all
this is somehow annoying and distracting because, after all, this
is a story of a monster with a disarming smile.

One of the most admired of all true crime stylists, Richard
Whittington-Egan, has written of this case, that in 1955, when a
book on the case appeared: 'Oddly, old Hay folk speak of him,
not as a murderer, but with affection as a sort of benefactor.
They rise fiercely to his defence if a stranger ... shows lack
of proper respect for his memory. They speak out strongly of
his many acts of goodwill and kindness.' It is almost as if, thirty
years after the criminal events around Armstrong and his
victims, the villainy was outweighed by the man's civic standing. He was a mason as well as a general all round 'good sort'.
His predilection for murder was apparently seen by some as a
mere aberration.

Some famous murders are of this character. To understand
this one, we have to travel back in imagination to 1910, when
Herbert Rowse Armstrong moved to his new home, Mayfield,
in Cusop Dingle, with his wife Katherine and their three children. We have to make an effort to call to mind what this man
was like and where he came from. The man lived very well in
Hay, with a housekeeper and a maid. With his large garden, he
could spend time outside, away from the wife who nagged. He
was tiny – barely 5 feet tall – but worked hard on his military
bearing. He had been a Volunteer and a Territorial, and
although he did briefly go over the France, most of the Great
War for Armstrong was in English depots. But he came back
from his part in the war and settled back into practice as a
solicitor. He had read law at Cambridge, and was then admitted
as a solicitor in 1895. His first experience in that profession had
been in Newton Abbot, where he was born in 1870, and then in

Liverpool. When he came to settle in Hay his rival was the firm run by Mr Griffiths.

Griffiths was in Armstrong's mind as he nurtured his ambition: he wanted the two companies to amalgamate. But as Mr Griffiths became ill, he took on Mr Oswald Martin, and in 1920, Griffiths died. Martin, who was wounded severely in the war, was left with a severe facial tic; he was clearly a competent man in his profession and he became a partner in the Griffiths business. The first biographers of Bernard Spilsbury, Browne and Tullet, pointed out back in 1952 that as Armstrong tried to become friendly with Martin and developed his standing in the town, there was a notorious murder case quite close at hand: Harold Greenwood, also a solicitor, was on trial in Carmarthen, and he was charged with poisoning his wife with arsenic. He was acquitted, but Browne and Tullet point out: 'The result must have been in Armstrong's thoughts when he made that last purchase of arsenic, on 11 January, at the shop of his rival's prospective father-in-law, Mr Davies, the chemist.'

Armstrong, the keen gardener, was at war with weeds. As was common at the time, arsenic was used in weedkiller and Davies the chemist was familiar with Armstrong's habits of using such a weedkiller in a tube with which he targeted dandelions. At the same time as these purchases, Mrs Armstrong was ill, and was deteriorating. The doctor who examined her thought that she was mentally ill, and her attitudes to Herbert had included a repressive regime which may have been partly a result of her mental anguish. He was forced to stay away from strong drink and he could smoke only in one designated room. Some writers have described her as a 'crack' and others as a 'terror' who made Herbert noticeably hen-pecked and was observed as so by the neighbours.

By August 1920, Katherine's health was indeed cause for concern. Medical advice was followed: she was taken away to a private asylum in Gloucester. Katherine was there for six months, and then when she returned home she was ill again, and in February 1921, she died. Armstrong stood to collect £2,300 by her death, but he was still short of cash, and he owed Martin £500 which had earlier been paid to Armstrong by a client in a land sale transaction. This situation made relations between Armstrong and Martin even more strained.

Now that Mrs Armstrong was no longer at home – and she could not object to the clothes he wore – Martin could visit Armstrong. He did, and he was offered buttered scones. The Major's words, 'Excuse fingers,' as he served the food to his guest, have since reached the status of one of those iconic statements from great crime stories – the polite and mannered words masking the fact that the scones had been injected with arsenic contained in the applicator for treating dandelions. Martin felt very ill after the tea-time chat, and matters escalated. Suspicions were aroused and a Dr Hincks was brought in. The Martins also received a box of chocolates, delivered by post, a present from Armstrong. Sure enough, Mrs Martin, who ate a chocolate, was violently sick. Putting two and two together, Martin made a case for attempted murder, and thoughts turned to Mrs Armstrong and how she may have conceivably died.

Armstrong was now investigated, and the medical men started a process which would lead to the exhumation of Katherine Armstrong. The moment is a very dramatic one: the great forensic scientist, Sir Bernard Spilsbury, made the journey from London to Hay on 2 January 1922. What had raised suspicions even more was the fact that Armstrong was in the habit of keeping small quantities of arsenic in screwed up parcels of brown paper. He would keep these in his pockets and in his desk drawers. When first questioned by police, they were aware of this, and of the fact that he had regularly bought arsenic from Mr Davies. Davies, Hincks and Martin must have had long and exploratory conversations about Armstrong before action was taken.

Spilsbury had conducted the investigation of Mrs Armstrong's corpse under a tent in the churchyard, and he had taken away several specimens for analysis. When it came to the process of investigation and eventually the charge of murder against Armstrong in April 1922 the trial opened at Hereford Assizes. Sir Henry Curtis-Bennett defended Armstrong and Mr Justice Darling presided. For the prosecution, Sir Ernest Pollock led for the Crown. Armstrong was on remand in prison at Gloucester and every day of the trial he was driven to Hereford and back. The trial was a momentous one for the great judge Darling. He was seventy-three and it was his last murder trial. Curtis-Bennett was a very astute man and a skilful speaker in court. All this made for this being one of the great criminal trials – and this escalated the status of the affair in the annals of murder in Britain.

Spilsbury's evidence was totally convincing and impressive. The chemist told the court that just before Mrs Armstrong came home from the asylum, the Major bought arsenic, and it seems that the chemist was remiss, in that he perhaps did not mix the arsenic with charcoal as he was supposed to do. Some coloured white arsenic was found on Armstrong's person, and then a second search of his desk revealed another arsenic parcel trapped at the back of a drawer – something that had been missed in the first police search. The stage was set for the conclusive evidence of Spilsbury. He told the court:

> From the amount of arsenic which was present in the small and large intestines it is clear that a large dose of arsenic must have been taken – I mean, a poisonous dose, possibly a fatal dose – certainly within twenty-four hours of death; and from the amount of arsenic which was found in the liver – over 2 grains – and from the disease which I found in the liver, it is clear that poison must have been given in a number of large doses extending over a period, certainly of some days, probably not less than a week . . .

The centre point of sheer sensation and puzzling interest was the fact that the packet of arsenic had been discovered at the back of the desk drawer in Armstrong's office. The defence, led by Curtis Bennett, appear to have used this as a gambit. One opinion is that it was placed there by the defence but that is a very cynical allegation. More likely is the possibility that Armstrong recalled that it was there and he told his defence team. The packet was two-faced though: Lord Darling thought the discovery was very damaging evidence, and both sides waited with bated breath for Armstrong himself to take the stand. What happened was that the court was asked to accept that Armstrong had the habit of poisoning each dandelion in his garden individually with a tool having a fine point.

The defence had to find a way to explain away that odd fact – not only that Armstrong used the tool with the fine point on the weeds, but that small holes had been found in poisoned chocolates which were surely the result of the use of that same tool. Curtis Bennett tried his best in his last speech to the jury, but nevertheless, according to those present, such as Filson Young who wrote about the case later, the general feeling was that Armstrong would be acquitted. This was wrong. Bennett actually went for a walk while the jury were out, and he expected to come back to a not guilty verdict. But Armstrong was found guilty and was sentenced to death.

Young mentions a story current at the time, and given in the popular press, about the jury: that there had been eleven statements of guilty on scraps of paper written by the jury, and one that said, 'Not proven'. As Young relates: '... when the foreman announced the result the man who had written "not proven" said, "Well Tom, you know what not proven means. I really believe the man is guilty". After which the foreman is alleged to have said, "We have heard enough of the case and we needn't discuss it any more. Let's have a quiet smoke before we go back into court."'

When he was asked if he had anything to say before sentence was passed, the little Major said simply, 'No, nothing.'

At the appeal court, Lord Hewart presided and he and his fellow judges had to endure a long and tedious speech by Bennett, covering a wide range of previous murder cases. They interrupted Bennett several times, and at last Hewart simply said,

> There is the clearest possible evidence that Armstrong, on 11 January, purchased a quarter of a pound of white arsenic, and that when he was arrested, on 31 December, he had in his pocket a packet containing a fatal dose of white arsenic. In these circumstances, as soon as he stated his defence – that he bought and was keeping the poison for the innocent purpose of destroying weeds – it was open to the prosecution to show by means of the evidence relating to Martin that Armstrong neither bought nor kept the poison for that pretended innocent purpose ...

The appeal was dismissed, as Hewart said, it raised 'no new principles of law; it elucidates no new aspect of familiar principles ...' The plain fact was that Armstrong was to hang. The date for his execution was set for 31 May 1922 and Rochdale hangman John Ellis was asked if he was available. Ellis, a racing man, knew that the date was Derby day; he also had another hanging date in the diary – he was due to hang the tall ex-soldier Hiram Thompson the day before. He arranged to leave Strangeways prison immediately after the first job, taking a train to Gloucester to hang Armstrong. As for his bet on the Derby, a warder put the bet on for him.

Armstong, as we have seen was very tiny man, and to make Ellis's job more difficult, the prisoner had not been weighed for three weeks. His weight had to be calculated to that Ellis could calculate the drop required from the scaffold. He was weighed, and he was just 8 stones 3 pounds, so the drop would have to be very deep – just 4 inches short of 9 feet. In Ellis's memoirs, there is a sidelight which throws a great deal of relevant knowledge about Armstrong. It relates to his reputation in the Welsh Marches and Herefordshire. Ellis wrote:

> When I went to Gloucester prison to hang him, the first words spoken to me there were by an official, who said, 'I hope you'll be as gentle as possible with Armstrong. He isn't an ordinary man.' For a moment I was absolutely stunned. The suggestion implied that I was in the habit of treating condemned men in a cruel way, and second, that Armstrong was entitled to some sort of special treatment. Can anyone wonder that I was resentful of such imputations?

Ellis, touchy and proud, formed an opinion of the man:

> Although he was only charged with the murder of his wife, I happen to know that if that case had failed there was enough evidence about the deaths of other people to have him hanged three times. This was the man they wanted me to be tender with.

The dapper, confident Armstrong whose photo has come down to us as a man with a flower in his button-hole and a warm smile, a man of military bearing, disappeared after the sentence, as Ellis noted: 'The hideous arrow-marked clothes seemed to bring home to him the truth ... he was in a state

of total dejection.' However, Armstrong had the required for-
titude when his hour came. Ellis recalled: 'To give Armstrong
his due, he went bravely to his death. Immediately he reached
my side I whipped the white cap over his head and fastened the
noose. Just as I put my hand on the lever I heard him speak his
last words, "I am coming, Kate!"'

CHAPTER 3

Jeannie Donald: Not Proven

The accused was in possession of sacks, similar to that in which the body was found . . .

William Roughead

This has to be the classic template case of lingering doubt, theory and supposition. It has the added dimension of interest we find in stories embedded in the ordinary, and in which the suspicious death at the heart of the enigma was never satisfactorily explained by forensic enquiry. The murder of Helen Priestly, eight and a half years old, in April 1934, in Urquhart Road, Aberdeen, appears to be resigned to the 'unsolved' category, in spite of the best minds in criminal analysis being applied to the known facts. Even the great William Roughead, doyen of true crime writers, admitted that all that was left, after the facts were given and the evidence assessed, was a puzzle, albeit one that offered a temptation for commentators and criminologists to apply their own thoughts.

Helen's body was found after a night's searching in the lobby of her parents' home in the tenements, and she was in a sack, with her feet projecting out; the sack had not been in the lobby at two in the morning of that day, and it was first discovered around five, after hope had almost gone that the girl would be found. She had been sexually interfered with, and there had been a reported cry of 'She's been used!' from someone during the chaos of the discovery and the gathering crowd that wanted to be present at the gruesome scene.

The story begins with Helen being sent out by her mother to buy a loaf of bread. She did not return and a search began. Jeannie Donald lived with her husband and daughter in the flat below the Priestly family. The neighbours searched around the street for hours, and Jeannie later said that she had been out at a local pavilion fair with her daughter, all evening until 11.00pm. In spite of the apparent alibi of all members – Mr Donald being at work that day, as a hairdresser, Jeannie was arrested and charged.

There was a police operation, and the green area behind the tenement was inspected for footprints; then of course the body and the sack were studied. Several famous scientists were involved in that work, including the charismatic Professor Sydney Smith. All the medical men found several details of great interest. There were cinders in the sack and in the child's mouth and hair. There were some small traces of blood there too. The cause of death was asphyxia, but there was an interesting fact here: Helen had an enlarged thymus and any pressure on that would have easily caused death.

There were signs of apparent rape, but on closer inspection, a perforation of the lower bowel and other signs of injury by a smallish and thin object. Professor Glaister from Glasgow University was a specialist in hair analysis and he looked at hairs found in the sack, in the Donald hearth, and in a brush taken from Jeannie Donald while on remand. All the expert could say was that there was a striking similarity: he had no definite confidence in saying they were all from the same source: Helen Priestly. At the trial, as William Roughead wrote: 'A long and learned cross-examination by Mr Blades left the matter much where it was.'

But some work of much more significance came from the evidence given by Professor Mackie of Edinburgh who subsequently explained that a rare bacillus, coliform in nature, was present in the underwear of the dead girl and also in a cleaning cloth in the Donald household. He said in court: 'I have given this very careful consideration and it is my considered opinion that the findings I have stated are very suggestive that these cloths had been contaminated from the same source as bloodstains on the child's combinations.' He said he would recommend a 'public authority' when faced with this contrast, to take action, and if it were a disease, he would 'recommend action with equal confidence'. Fibres were also examined, by an expert from Bradford, and some found in the sack matched those in the Donald house; but the problem with that was that the

Donalds kept lots of sacks for cinders and other waste, and so such materials would be expected.

Far more useful were the findings of Sydney Smith, who was described by Roughead (who was at the trial) in this way: 'An ideal witness, alert but calm, positive but polite, clear, competent and urbane under the most rigorous cross-examination.' He had been the first to spot the coliform bacillus and he examined a large number of items from the Donald house; he looked at fibres and cinders and found matches. The wiping cloth had traces of vomit on it, and that was important later. Smith was also sure that the knickers were torn before there was bleeding, and that the child had at first been lying face-down. What all experts agreed on was that there had been no male rape.

This point was important because that had been taken as a strong possibility. A little boy told police that he had seen Helen being abducted by a man, but later he confessed that he had made up the tale. There was also the reported statement about a man hanging around the area. But several people who had been involved in the hunt for the girl later said that there had been no unusual sightings of unknown people as they looked around the whole area in the early hours of the morning.

The crucially vital details that pointed the finger of guilt at Jeannie Donald were that the light on her flat had been seen on at around 3.00am but no one from her family had come out to help; the sack from her flat, containing the body, had apparently been placed there later in the morning after the main search. There was no evidence of any other person present who could have done the killing. Jeannie Donald and Mrs Priestley, though they had no open confrontations nor anger expressed, did not speak to each other. Jeannie expressed the situation with these words: 'It was because of water coming down; we had no row, only we did not speak . . .' All this was fairly strong material to work with. Add to that the established fact that little Helen used to tease and annoy Jeannie in various ways, and the minutiae of the forensic evidence – such as the cinders on the body and in the sack and the mysterious disappearance of a box of ash from the floor in the Donalds' room, and things looked bleak for the accused.

If she were guilty, then it seemed that the body of the little girl must have been kept in the Donalds' flat somewhere for several hours – certainly from 11.30pm through to around 5.00am. That implied a callous and evil nature behind the reserved and quiet front that Mrs Donald put on for the world when questioned. When the accused was asked why there was no demonstrable involvement from her in the search for the girl and other matters pertaining to Helen, she replied that she had given a shilling towards a wreath. When, in the early hours when the body had been found, a neighbour had said to Jeannie that, 'They are thinking that she met her death here ... it was some person about the door ...' Jeannie had said nothing, but simply gone inside her own rooms.

Before leaving for the pavilion with her daughter, Jeannie said that, in the afternoon, two suspicious and disreputable men had called at her house. One she said was a dirty, unshaven old man with his hands in his pockets. It all seems rather weak and stereotyped. But on the final day of the trial there was anew witness, and the defence counsel, Mr Blades, said that at 3.30pm, on the afternoon of the killing, a teenager had seen what she thought was a tramp walking with a little girl who had a blue dress, a tammy hat and black stockings. She was also carrying a parcel suggestive of a loaf and she seemed 'scared like'. But this had been already looked into earlier, and there was a suspicion of yet another fabrication.

When the court process was complete, matters were looking bad for Mrs Donald. There were no other suspects and no other related lines of thought. Some things he could use were actions such as a police surgeon who had said that blood was found in the Donald flat but he later changed his mind, and also that the forensics had not been conclusive. The alibi for the afternoon – that Mrs Donald and her daughter had been to the pavilion and had also been shopping at a market – was not contested and no witnesses were called to say yes or no to that claim.

But in the end, as the Lord Advocate reminded everyone in his summing-up, the evidence from Professors Mackie and Smith about the bacillus was hard to deny. There was also the strange business of the Donald's light being on at 3.00am and their absence from the search. The latter point must have been a formative detail in the general condemnation of the accused.

It took less than twenty minutes for the jury to reach a decision. There are fifteen people in a Scottish jury and in this case, thirteen found Mrs Donald guilty of murder and two decided it was not proven.

The death sentence stated that Mrs Donald 'be hanged in the prison of Aberdeen on 13 August . . .' But there was an appeal for clemency and for the sentence to be commuted to prison for life. This was done by means of 1926 legislation: The Criminal Appeal (Scotland) Act. This laid down that an appeal had to be lodged within ten days of the sentence, and so the lawyers lost no time, and when the response came from the Scottish office in London it was favourable for the condemned:

> With reference to the case of Jeannie Ewen or Donald, now lying under sentence of death in His Majesty's Prison, Aberdeen, I have to inform you that, after full consideration, I have felt justified in advising His Majesty to respite the execution of the capital sentence, with a view to its commutation to penal servitude for life.

The life was spared but the mystery remains. It is hard not to agree with William Roughead, who sees the solution as being a case of anger on the part of Jeannie Donald, after being once again teased by the girl who called her 'Cocoanut' and banged on her door. Was it just a temper that went too far and a shaking at the neck did damage to the girl with the enlarged thymus gland? Everything after that would be explained by a need to cover up the actual accidental death with signs of attack and rape.

It was in the end, perhaps, a tale of the last straw in a long line of childish torments. Then, all the actions (or lack of action) by the women in the flat downstairs could be interpreted as the hard, disgusting deeds of a killer rather than as the silence of a terrified criminal who knew that she had done something seriously wrong and that the world must not know the truth. We don't know the truth today, but the theory of accidental death, on a fragile little girl, makes sense.

With regard to the general view of execution on women, this reprieve was not unusual: there had been others as attitudes changed, but only six months after this case, Ethel Major was hanged in Hull prison for poisoning her husband in the little Lincolnshire village of Kirby-on-Bain. Britain was not such a civilised country after all, many thought that Christmas when the death was reported in the press. Naturally, in Aberdeen, there were many who had no problem with hangings, and they were sorely disappointed that Mrs Donald did not swing on the gallows for killing 'one of their own'.

CHAPTER 4

Lily's Story

I did not know my husband had died from strychnine poisoning.

Ethel Major

On February 2010, I stood in Hull prison, staring at the death cell and the execution suite just across the corridor, on 'twos' as the second level is called in prison parlance. The bare cell still has the stone slab. I imagined a straw mattress but maybe that was too melodramatic. Then I took in the few steps required for the hangman's victim to be taken, pinioned, from that box to the small space across from the door in which the trapdoor would have been, ready for the convict to be stretched and the body dropped down to ground level. I also noticed, above me, and placed in such a way that someone looking could see anyone walking around outside the cell, there was a small window. This is where the executioner would have watched Ethel Major, a small, thin woman. He would have looked and assessed her body weight, to help calculate the length of drop required when he hanged her. He did just that, five days before Christmas Day in 1934.

I shuddered as I looked at this so-called 'suite.' That word has to be the most sick and nasty euphemism in the language.

There are dozens of reasons for calling this case the most significant and contentious in the history of crime in Lincolnshire. Reappraisals of the reasons why Ethel Major was hanged for the murder of her husband when she mounted the scaffold in Hull prison a few days before Christmas 1934 have been made regularly over the years. The problem is that nothing can turn the clock back, and re-examining this case is a painful business.

The outline of the case is reasonably straightforward, but a controversy will follow. The Majors, lorry driver Arthur and wife Ethel, lived in Kirkby-on-Bain near Horncastle with their fifteen-year-old son. They were not happily married; she was forty-two and her husband forty-four. Arthur had a drink problem and he was very difficult to live with. He also appeared to be having an affair with a neighbour, a Mrs Kettleborough, and Ethel said that she had seen two love letters written by this woman to her husband. Hard though it is to believe in hindsight, Ethel Major showed these to her family doctor and said these words to him: 'A man like that is not fit to live, and I will do him in.'

Arthur Major died as a result of what was defined as an epileptic fit, but then, before the funeral could take place, this anonymous letter arrived on the desk of Inspector Dodson of Horncastle police:

> Sir, have you ever heard of a wife poisoning her husband? Look further into the death (by heart failure) of Mr Major of Kirkby-on-Bain. Why did he complain of his food tasting nasty and throw it to a neighbour's dog, which has since died? Ask the undertaker if he looked natural after death? Why did he stiffen so quickly? Was he so jerky when dying? I myself have heard her threaten to poison him years ago. In the name of the law, I beg you to analyse the contents of his stomach.

This was signed, 'Fairplay'. A coroner's order stopped the interment and Major's body was examined again. The coffin was actually removed in the presence of the mourners. Ethel was in her house with relatives, including Arthur's two brothers, when the police arrived. 'It looks as though they're suspicioning me' she told her father, and he agreed. Ethel, small, spectacled and short-sighted, was an unassuming woman with some quirky habits and a complicated nature.

It soon emerged that indeed the dog, a wire-haired fox terrier, had died after having muscular spasms. The pathologist, Dr Roche Lynch of St Mary's Hospital, Paddington, also confirmed that Arthur Major's body had the quantity of strychnine sufficient to kill the man. On examination, the surface of his body was blue, and almost any contact on the skin would initiate a spasm. Arthur's body had 1.27 grains in it and the dog had 0.12 grains. The average fatal dose for a man was between 1 and 2 grains. Lynch opined that Major had taken two doses:

one on 22 May and the fatal one on 24 May. To dismiss any possibility of suicide, Lynch said, 'On account of the awful agony he would go through, I do not think that any would-be suicide would take it a second time, unless he were insane.'

It had been a terrible and agonising death. His son Lawrence saw Arthur walking into the front room with his head between his hands, then as the man went outside, Lawrence saw him fall over. He was put to bed, and when Tom Brown came later, he saw Arthur foaming at the mouth and in the throes of violent spasms. Later, when Dr Smith came, he made up his mind that this was epilepsy. It was going to be a long process of dying for the man, and in court it was revealed that Ethel had left him alone for the night, then in the following morning, she had gone shopping. Later in the day he seemed to recover and he actually drank some tea, but then there was a relapse. Virtually the last words Arthur Major spoke to his wife were, 'You have been good to me.'

Ethel Major was interviewed by Chief Inspector Hugh Young of Scotland Yard, and he has given an account of her in which she stated that her husband had died of eating some corned beef. 'She appeared over-eager to impress me with the fact that she had nothing to do with providing his meals, explaining that for a fortnight before her husband's death she and her son had stayed with her father ...' Young was eager to point out that Ethel was a cool and resourceful woman and that she 'showed no pangs of sorrow at the loss of her husband'.

The crucially important statement made by Ethel to Young was, 'I did not know my husband had died from strychnine poisoning' and Young replied, 'I never mentioned strychnine poisoning. How did you know that?' As H Montgomery Hyde pointed out in his biography of Lord Birkett, that in Birkett's time poisoning 'was considered such a repulsive crime that convicted prisoners were practically never reprieved'.

When Ethel Major was arrested and charged, the full story emerged and Lord Birkett, talented as he was, knew that he would lose this case. There was too much evidence against her. At Lincoln Assizes, on 30 October 1934, she appeared before Mr Justice Charles. Richard O'Sullivan and P E Sandlands prosecuted, and Ethel pleaded not guilty.

One of the most convincing pieces of evidence against her was the fact that she had a key belonging to a chest her father, Tom Brown, used to store strychnine; this was used to kill vermin. Tom Brown testified that he had lost the key to his chest some years before and that he had had a new key made. When Sandlands brought out a key, Brown confirmed that it was the one he had lost. This key had been in Ethel Major's possession. There was also a hexagonal green bottle for storing strychnine; this had been found in the Majors' house. Then came further information about the access Ethel had to her father's house. She had known where a key was hidden outside, and a purse she had containing the key to the chest was confirmed as being one that belonged to her mother.

Tom Brown was questioned about this key. Here is a point of real fascination: the father was testifying against his daughter. Lord Birkett must have seen this as another nail in the coffin for his already flimsy defence. There he was in the witness box, a whiskered old countryman. Regarding the key, the prosecution pointed out that the last key had turned up 'shining as though it had been recently polished' in Ethel Major's possession. Birkett desperately tried to retrieve the situation by saying that lots of women carried trivial objects and mementos around in their handbags. In other words, she may have had the purse and key, but not the strychnine. Tom Brown had looked at the little bottle and suggested that it seemed to have the same amount in it as it had had the last time he looked at it.

The heart of the situation was the strychnine and the corned beef she knew was her husband's last meal. Ethel had admitted that she knew some corned beef in the cupboard was not really edible and yet she had left it, saying nothing to anyone. She had known Arthur was due to eat it. Looking into the tale of the corned beef was to be important in court. Contradictory things were said about the purchase of the tin of beef, Ethel saying Arthur had sent Lawrence to buy it, and Lawrence saying the opposite. All this cast doubt on Ethel's statement, though it has to be said that the retailer recalled that Lawrence had come for the beef and said that his father had given him the money to buy it.

Tom Brown did, however, have quite a lot to say about Arthur Major's character, relating that when Brown's first wife had died in 1929, Arthur had come to the Majors' place very drunk and had used threatening words. Ethel Major's daughter, Auriel Brown, was asked about the love letters and the supposed affair Arthur was having with Mrs Kettleborough. Birkett knew that if there was to be any chink in the armour of the prosecution's case, it was going to be in the possibility of provocation with regard to this affair. The focus of their dialogue was not promising in this respect:

> Mr Birkett: 'Did you ever see anything that you thought suspicious between Mrs Kettleborough and Major?'
> Auriel: 'I saw them once making eyes at each other. Mrs Kettleborough was always outside the house when Major came home. She put herself in his way.'
> Mr Birkett: 'The advances that you saw were on one side?'
> Auriel: 'Both sides.'

A great deal more information about the Majors' life together was to emerge. They hated the very sight of each other. Arthur Major had severe financial problems and he was of the opinion that his wife was a spendthrift and was helping to ruin him. Only a few days before he died, Arthur Major had placed an announcement in the local paper, the *Horncastle News*, removing himself for any responsibility in debts his wife had accrued. The situation at No.2 council houses was far worse than many around the village would have suspected.

One fundamental cause of their rift was the fact that Ethel, before she met Arthur, had given birth to a child (Auriel) in 1914, when she was only twenty-three. She never revealed the name of the father, and the girl was brought up as a daughter of the Browns. This refusal to give details of the business infuriated Arthur; things deteriorated so much that she left him for a while, going back home to the family home.

In court at Lincoln, Lord Birkett wrote later, he knew the verdict of the jury when they came back into court after an hour's deliberation; none of them looked in the direction of Ethel Major. They found her guilty, but with a recommendation for mercy. Ethel collapsed and moaned that she was innocent as she was carried away.

There was a sure feeling that a formal appeal was a waste of time; but Birkett did join a group of lawyers who petitioned the Home Secretary for a reprieve. The response was that there was 'insufficient grounds to justify him in advising His Majesty to interfere with the due course of law'. One last ditch appeal came from the Lord Mayor of Hull, in the form of a telegram to the King and Queen, pleading for their intervention.

On 19 December, Ethel Major was executed by Thomas Pierrepoint, with the Under Sheriff of Lincolnshire present. As usual, the Governor, Captain Roberts, made the statement about the hanging being done in 'a humane and expeditious manner'.

Yet in many ways, this is only the beginning of the Ethel Major story. After all, the sentence was based on circumstantial evidence and there were certainly factors of provocation, an argument that she was not her normal self when she acted, and that there was considerable enmity and aggression towards her from her husband.

A more close and searching account of Ethel Major's life is helpful in understanding these events, and also in seeing why there have been so many reassessments of the case. She was born Ethel Brown in Monkton Bottom, Lincolnshire, in 1891. Her father was a gamekeeper and they lived on the estate of Sir Henry Hawley. By all accounts she lived a good life as a child, with her three brothers and parents, going to a small school at Coningby and then at Mareham-le-Fen. She stayed at home for some years, learning dressmaking and the usual domestic skills. But after came the liaison with the unknown lover and her pregnancy. Some writers make something of this with regard to her later criminality; it has been pointed out that of eight women hanged in Britain in significant cases, five had illegitimate children. That doesn't have any real significance, but it illustrates the need some writers on crime have to find patterns and profiles.

Ethel had known Arthur Major when they were children. In 1907, he left the area to live in Manchester, but then, in the Great War, he joined the Manchester Regiment and they began to meet. When he was wounded and hospitalised back home, in Bradford, they wrote to each other. Keeping the truth about Auriel quiet until they were married was perhaps the basic error in her understanding of her new husband's personality. In court, in 1934, there was to be a great deal said about potential provocation on the part of Arthur Major, and even more written in years to come.

Birkett cross-examined Lawrence in an attempt to provide a clearer picture of Arthur Major's character traits. Lawrence confirmed that his father came home drunk almost every night and that this was becoming more severe in recent months. The topic then shifted to violence and fear:

> Birkett: 'When he was in that state, did he quarrel violently with your mother?'
> Lawrence: 'Yes, if we were in.'

When wife and son did retreat to Tom Brown's, they would sleep on a couch in the kitchen or in a garden shed, Lawrence sleeping in his topcoat and all his day-clothes. A story began to emerge that would, in other times and places, be part of a full picture of provocation and mitigating circumstances. In 1931, Ethel Major had taken out a summons for separation, so violent had his behaviour been. Arthur made vows to reform his life and Ethel changed her mind. Tom Brown had confirmed that 'Major used violent and filthy language to his wife and also threatened her.'

As in most marital situations of such conflict, questions will be asked about the nature of the relationship and whether or not there really was a victim and an aggressor. At this trial, Judge Charles and indeed Norman Birkett used this approach. Birkett boldly asked young Lawrence, 'Should I be right in saying that your mother all your life has been very kind to you, and your father very wicked?' Judge Charles went ahead and asked witnesses in general about where blame might lie.

Therefore we have questions such as, 'What sort of a fellow was Major?' and 'Did you ever see him the worse for liquor?' One could guess the outcome of this. People such as the vicar's wife and the rector talked of Major as 'sober' as far as they knew. He was a man with a very amiable public persona; yet inside his own home he was often monstrous to his own family.

If we turn to the other element in potential defence of provocation, the subject of the love letters comes up. What exactly was the truth about Arthur Major and his affair? We need to recall here that Major was many things in the village: not only voluntary work for the church but time put in as a local councillor. Ethel's report was that she found some love letters in their bedroom, and of course this has the implication that she had been searching for evidence after so much innuendo and whispering about an 'affair'. One such was this, which was read out in court:

> To my dearest sweetheart,
> In answer to your dear letter received this morning, thank you dearest. The Postman was late I was waiting a long time for him ... I see her watching you in the garden ... Well, sweetheart, I will close with fondest love to my precious one ...
>   From your loving sweetheart,
>   ROSE

When she faced Arthur with her new knowledge (she had already told her doctor, Dr Armour) he said he would do nothing. The issue became a cause and a local crusade for Ethel; she wrote complaints about her husband to the local police and even tried to change the terms of the leasehold of their property so that she could be classed as a 'tenant'. The natural end of this was a talk with a solicitor, and a letter was drafted, as she said, on behalf of her husband, warning Mrs Rose Kettleborough not to write again. This solicitor had witnessed Major making violent threats against Ethel, but not taken it to be anything serious.

The Kettleboroughs in court provide a record of what can only be called tittle-tattle, and some of the discussion of the case on record seems entirely trivial; yet when Rose herself took the stand, there was clearly something interesting to come. In her fur coat, this small, attractive woman said that she had never 'been out' with Arthur Major. She also denied loitering to wait for Arthur by the house, as Auriel had said.

When the subject of the letters came up, Birkett tried very hard to do some amateur handwriting analysis, comparing her orthography and style in the love letters to other writing she had done. Nothing was achieved by this, and even an exploration of her past knowledge of Arthur led to nothing significant. To sum up, Birkett had attempted every ploy he could think of, but in the end, the record of the trial can be made to read more like an indulgence in small scale scandal than a murder case.

But this is not the end of the saga of Ethel major. A study of the case by Annette Ballinger in 2000 takes a closer look at the provocation line of thought. In her book, *Dead Women Walking* (2000), Ballinger pays attention to comments made at the time about the discontent in the Major home, such as the statement by a solicitor's clerk that 'Arthur often threatened his wife. I gather that their home life was unhappy.' She also puts great emphasis on the change in Major as he drank more. His son's words that 'The drink was having an effect on my father, he was not the man he had been' do imply an almost submerged narrative that has only been re-examined closely since this sad affair came to a close.

For Ballinger, it was the issue of the right to remain silent that shaped Ethel's destiny. The factors which stood most prominently in court – the fact that the day before Major's death he had withdrawn from responsibility for her debts, and her husband's apparent condition of being a poor victim – made her silence worse. As Ballinger notes: '... the case of Ethel Major demonstrates how the prisoner's right to remain silent could be interpreted as evidence of guilt. Thus the judge referred to Ethel's non-appearance in the witness box no less than six times in his summing up.

The 1898 Criminal Evidence Act had made the 'right to silence' concept very important in the construction of defences. But unfortunately, the unforeseen side-effects were that juries would tend to interpret silence as guilt in many cases. This would be despite the fact that some people in the dock would be nervous, apprehensive, or even in some cases, would have been advised by their brief to say nothing.

Ballinger sees Ethel Major as a 'battered woman' and notes that generally such women are too traumatised to give evidence. But there was no militant, prominent feminist movement in the inter-war years, of course. One common view, and this is something that helps us understand Ethel Major's situation, is that, according to Lind Gordon, 'wife beating became part of a general picture of slovenly behaviour, associated with drunkenness, and squalor of the wife's own making'.

Finally, if the notion of Ethel's failure to safeguard her reputation is on the agenda in this notorious case, then aspects of
her behaviour in the village have to be an important factor in
understanding how she was perceived and judged in court. Her
eccentric questioning of various neighbours, her interviews with
the doctor, and her letters to the press, all add up to a picture of
a woman who was both desperate and indeed in a very nervous
state. The documented behaviour of this woman as she worked
hard to put things right in the household only made her situation worse. Of course, in court, these actions would be seen as
reinforcing the moral condemnation of her as someone who
had, earlier in her life, had an illegitimate child and not told her
husband about it.

Part of the judgement on her was also that she was generally
bad tempered, and this was made more prominent than her
husband's equally capricious and aggressive behaviour. On one
occasion she had thrown a brick and had 'embarked on a wild
round of revenge and malice that included half the population
of the village', according to another commentary on the case.

The executioner at the time, Albert Pierrepoint, wrote about
the other way women killers need to be seen: not as the hard,
rational poisoners of the media images, but as 'ordinary
women, rarely beautiful ... square faced, thin mouthed, eyes
blinking behind National Health glasses ... hair scraped thin
by curlers, lumpy ankles above homely shoes ...' As Annette
Ballinger has said, '... poison was responsible for her death'.
By that she means that the nature of that specific version of
homicide carries with it a discourse and a media amplification
going back centuries, as something that has entered folklore.
When Ethel Major's case started covering the main pages of
newspapers, the whole back-list of women poisoners was
invoked. All the images of women using arsenic on husbands,
from Mary Ann Cotton back in the mid Victorian times, to the
earlier Lincolnshire instances, were on the stage as the sad story
unfolded. For decades, the pages of the *Police Gazette* had been
full of lurid tales of women poisoners; what hope was there for
truth to emerge when the media had categorised them as the
worst kind of heartless killers?

Alderman Stark of Hull, when he wrote a last appeal for
clemency, saying, 'For the sake of humanity I implore you to

reconsider your decision, especially having regard to the nearness of Christmas ... The heartfelt pleas contained in this telegram are those of 300,000 inhabitants and particularly those of the women of this great city', was fighting more than a judicial decision. He was going against the grain of many centuries of myths around the 'women are more deadly than the male' notion.

The sense of defeat and the inevitable conclusion on the scaffold was hovering over her defence from the beginning. Lord Birkett's memoirs contain his view that Crown Counsel had opened with a statement that had a ring of finality: '... the case is really on the evidence unanswerable'. One of the very best defence lawyers in the land could do nothing. It seems odd with this in mind that the *Daily Express* had insisted that 'Nobody believes she will be hanged', just a few weeks before the sentence.

There was no way that an appeal based on the unfairness of the judge's summing up would succeed. Whoever 'Fairplay' was who sent the anonymous letter, he or she had opened the path to the gallows for Ethel Major, and the only consolation, looking back over the years, is that the Pierrepoints were very skilled men in their trade. Ethel would have left this world very speedily indeed, though they must have felt something similar to John Ellis when he hanged Edith Thompson in 1922: 'My own feelings defy description ... I kept telling myself that the only humane course was to work swiftly and cut her agony as short as possible.' This is a stark reminder of what feelings were with James Berry when he dealt with Mary Lefley, in 1884.

Unfortunately, in spite of all the above discussion of this fascinating case study, the reference books will always have the same kind of simplified statements for the record, as these words from Gaute and O'Dell's *The Murderers' Who's Who* (1979): 'Major, Ethel Lillie. A forty-three-year-old Lincolnshire gamekeeper's daughter who murdered her husband with strychnine.' The woman who never gave evidence at her trial is being judged by posterity, still enveloped in silence. In modern terms, and with a more feminist, open-minded view of *mens rea*, the mind-set to take a life, it can be argued that in 1934 there was a too narrow definition of intention, because the accused is supposed to see the same probability that the jury do, in the way that the intention is given to them by lawyers interpreting the defendant's actions.

But all that would have been far too subtle for the court in Ethel Major's case. For anyone with a belief in the possibility of paranormal events, it must be said that the story of Ethel Major, in a sense, goes on. Several officers in HMP Hull have reported seeing a woman's spirit walking the landing where Ethel was hanged. Perhaps most convincing in this is that she had become accepted: new officers are usually expected to report seeing a ghost and the response is usually, 'Oh that's just Mrs Major.'

CHAPTER 5

The Bryant Poisoning Case

The coward's weapon, poison . . .

Phineas Fletcher

The old adage that 'whatever nourishes me, destroys me' could be applied to any of the seven deadly sins, but it fits lust perfectly. Charlotte Bryant, had she the education to reflect on such literary texts, would have seen how those words applied to her as she sat in the condemned cell in Exeter jail in 1936. Her pursuit of a travelling man while still married to her dairyman, John, led to her desire to remove the husband from the scene with the help of some weedkiller.

This case was one of many involving arsenic in the 1920s and 1930s. Like Armstrong and like Ethel Major, Charlotte saw the answer to her problem in the weedkiller she could buy at the pharmacist. Since the first Arsenic Act of 1851 there had been attempts to regulate the sale of the poison; by the early twentieth century, the sale of white, as opposed to yellow, arsenical powder, sold in the pure state, meant that it had to be coloured with indigo to make it distinctive. But arsenic in other substances, such as the tin of Eureka weedkiller Charlotte bought, simply had to be sold to a known buyer and the sale recorded. When she went to buy the stuff she could only sign with an 'x', as she was illiterate. That purchase was the beginning of the end for the young woman from Derry who had married a soldier, John Frederick Bryant, and gone to settle in Coombe, near Sherborne.

Dying of arsenical poisoning has to be one of the most agonizing exits from the world we can imagine. The stuff has been the preference of killers down the centuries because it is easy to hide in food, having only a slightly sweet and metallic scent to it. But its effects are horrific. It is something which can be administered piecemeal, so being stored in the liver, and when the final and deadly dose is given, the terrible death

trajectory begins. The sensations experienced have been described as the sense of having a burning ball of hot metal in the
gut; on top of that, the victim has vicious diarrhoea, vomiting
and spasms in the joints, dizziness and consequent depression.

Frederick Bryant was to die in that way. But the Bryant story
begins long before 1936. The couple met in 1922 when Bryant
was serving as a military policeman in the Dorset Regiment. In
Derry, where he was stationed, Charlotte was well known
among the soldiers, being called 'Darkie' with reference to her
swarthy looks. She was keen on going out with soldiers, and
indeed risked being attacked by the republicans for that habit.
She was an 'easy lay', and no doubt earned cash by selling herself around the local military patch.

She was born in 1904, and Frederick was eight years older
than her. They married in Wells, Somerset and then moved into
Bryant's home county of Dorset where he found work as a farm
labourer. It is clear, with hindsight, that such a cultural shock,
going from being the centre of sexual attention from hordes of
squaddies to being a farm worker's wife in an isolated cottage,
was a recipe for disaster.

From the beginning, there is a rare peculiarity about this case.
That is in Bryant's tolerance of his wife carrying on her sexual
affairs in Dorset, and her behaviour being common knowledge.
She earned some cash from her sexual favours, and it is on
record (from the trial interviews) that Bryant said, 'I don't care
what she does. Four pounds a week is better than thirty
shillings!' Then, in December 1933, Charlotte met Leonard
Parsons, also known as Moss, a horse-trader. Not only did
Bryant not mind his wife putting it about around the village: he
allowed her new lover to settle into the family home and create
the classic *ménage a trois* from which so much grief and conflict
comes. At first the arrangement seems to have been amicable
and worked well, giving each person what they wanted from life.
But when it came to Frederick telling Parsons to leave, matters
became bitter. Charlotte began to realize that in order to keep
the man she really wanted, her husband would have to go.

In May 1935, Frederick was severely poorly after eating a
meal prepared by his wife. As he recovered a few days later, the
doctor ascribed the problem as being gastro-enteritis. Then in
August he was ill again, with the same symptoms of vomiting

and diarrhoea. Again he came back to health. But in November, the lover told Charlotte that he would have to leave, to find work elsewhere. This was probably the turning point for Charlotte, and in early December Frederick was ill again, and for a third time he recovered.

Charlotte was friendly with a woman called Ostler, and the latter was invited to come and live with the Bryants; the guest was to become a key witness. Just a few days before Christmas, Bryant was ill again. This time it was very serious; he was taken to Sherborne Hospital, where he died. It appears that he was considering signing off the panel and resuming work on 20 December, but on the afternoon of the following day he was much worse; the doctor who had treated him on the previous occasions made his suspicions of arsenical poisoning known to the police, and the doctor would not issue a death certificate.

A post mortem was done, and the coroner directed that the usual specimens be sent to Dr Roche Lynch, a forensic expert working with Scotland Yard. He had been working with the CID since 1920, when he was appointed assistant official analyst. We can see how thorough this was if we note the report of the man called in to lead the investigation – Inspector Arthur Bell. He listed the materials sent to Lynch: these included complete organs, including the stomach and contents, small and large intestines, urine in the bladder, vomit and excreta, complete lungs, portions of skin and hair, brain and nails. In addition, these were taken from the area around the body: samples of soil from above the coffin, below the coffin and from adjacent ground, sawdust from the coffin, and a portion of the shroud.

Lynch found plenty of evidence of arsenic, but while that was going on, Bell and other officers spent several days at the Bryants' home, searching for anything that would be a factor in proving the presence of arsenic. The Bryants had five children, ranging from fifteen months to fourteen years of age, and Mrs Ostler had two children. These were all removed to a Poor Law institution by the NSPCC. They were settled at the institution at Sturminster Newton. Bell went to the cottage and later reported:

> As an indication of the thoroughness with which the
> officers concerned carried out their distasteful work, it may

be mentioned that they were occupied in daylight hours for weeks ... dust was taken from shelves and cupboards, drawers, lino, mats, articles of furniture ... Samples of ashes, earth, rubbish and water were also taken. In all, more than 150 samples of dust, scrapings etc., were submitted to the analyst.

While Lynch was at work on the materials collected, Bell got to work on Charlotte: he said that there were two notable conclusions from his interviews with her; that she lied continually, and that she tried to implicate Mrs Ostler and cast suspicion on her. The police were determined in their search for arsenic and for anything which may have absorbed arsenic, watching every move Charlotte made, such as her request to cut her long and filthy fingernails. When she had done this, the cuttings were inspected but no traces were found. As Bell commented: 'It will be realized that if arsenic had been found it would have been very damaging to her defence.' She had a solicitor appointed, and so said nothing else to the detectives while investigations continued.

Then Mrs Ostler spoke to police and some intriguing information was given, notably that the two women had had a conversation about a tin of weedkiller. Bell explained this:

> She said that on the 24th December after the inquest, when Sergeant Taylor called for a bottle of medicine, Mrs Bryant asked Mrs Ostler the reason why the officer had called. Mrs Ostler replied to the effect that it was evident they found something in the body which ought not to have been there. Shortly afterwards, Mrs Bryant called her son into the outhouse to clear up some rubbish and also to clear that part of the garden near the rubbish heap. She also went to the cupboard in the room on the ground floor and from the bottom shelf she took a weedkiller tin ...

Behind this, she went on to say, there was another tin, a brand of weedkiller called Eureka. When Mrs Ostler asked what she had that for, Bryant said, 'I must get rid of this ... Don't you say anything. If nothing is found, they can't put a rope round your neck!'

Meanwhile, Roche Lynch was studying the materials and the body organs. The dust was found to have 58,000 parts per million of arsenic; 37 of the 153 articles taken from the cottage were found to have arsenic. From this, other conclusions were reached, such as the fact that dust taken from the right-hand pocket of the coat Charlotte said she had worn on the day she went supposedly for medicine was also found to have arsenic.

When, after a further search, the tin of Eureka weedkiller was found, partly burned, what was needed was some evidence that Charlotte had been to buy it. Police were hopeful when a chemist at Yeovil was found on whose register a sale of the substance was found on the register for the right date, and with a cross instead of a signature. The chemist said that he knew the woman who had come for the poison, but amazingly, he could not identify her, and even her Irish accent which should have been memorable to him, did not lodge in his mind and provide a positive identification. Bell was sure that Charlotte had 'bounced' the weedkiller from the young assistant in the shop, although she was a complete stranger. The assistant was possibly covering himself for not having been meticulous with his paperwork, recording and being observant in such a sale.

The police must have thought that they were stuck in a cul-de-sac in the pursuit of real evidence about the poison. But then more forensic information was forthcoming: soil naturally contains arsenic, as does coal, and the average proportion for that is 18 parts per million. In the soil just below the rubbish tip where there had been an attempt to burn the tin, the arsenic content was 73 parts per million. Ashes taken from that tip showed 92 parts per million.

The challenge then facing Inspector Bell was to study the manufacture of the tin. This was to prove that the partly burned tin was the same as the one on the shelf just before Christmas. Sergeant Tapsell was the man who went out to talk to the manufacturers; he found that the first maker looked at the tin and said it was not one of his, but at the second manufacturer, Tapsell, used Holmesian deduction:

> . . . by placing a sheet upside down . . . the girl operating the machine accepted it without question, with the result that it was locked in exactly the same way as the burnt tin. This

demonstration so convinced the manufacturer that . . . with conviction, he gave evidence that the tin was similar to those manufactured by his firm for the Eureka Weedkiller Company . . .

Bell and his team were tireless in their search for information about the Bryants, Parsons and other people who knew the family. Parsons was interviewed, but he had a sound alibi. Around 300 statements were taken, and from this persistent police work there came at last a valuable piece of evidence. A neighbour recalled that, earlier in the year, when Bryant had suffered one of the first attacks of sickness, he had taken some tea out to the field – tea prepared by Charlotte. He only remembered this while he was doing the same thing a year later.

Inspector Bell wrote that 'There was none of the so-called brilliant detective work in this case, but there was a lot of hard work done by loyal, enthusiastic, intelligent officers . . . The officers of the Dorset Constabulary were on excellent terms with all the local officials, from whom we readily received valuable assistance . . .' Bell's participation was unusual: it was the first time since the Great War period that the Met had gone to work in the shires.

Then, with evidence in place, Charlotte Bryant went to court. She stood in the dock at the Dorset Assizes on 29 May, 1936. Mr Justice MacKinnon presided; the defence was led by J D Casswell and the case for the Crown was led by Sir Terence O'Connor, who was the Solicitor General. Charlotte, aged thirty-three and with a very real threat of never seeing her next birthday birthday, pleaded not guilty.

Casswell's argument was that the jury must keep out of their minds the moral condemnation so easily applied to woman who not only '. . . slept around; but who lived with a lover under the same roof as her husband'. The barrister said, 'There is plenty of suspicion, but that falls very far short of evidence and a case for conviction.' Under questioning by Casswell, Charlotte's brief was to insist on her ignorance of any poison, and to try to have the incriminating Eureka tin discounted:

Mrs Bryant denied that there was a tin of weedkiller in the living room on the shelf. She denied also that she said, 'I must get rid of this' and that she took it away to destroy.

But then O'Connor aimed straight at the main issue:

> You know that after your husband died, large quantities of arsenic were found inside him, which would have been quite enough to cause any of the symptoms we have heard about?

Mrs Bryant replied, 'I do not know anything whatever, Sir, about arsenic.'

Casswell made much of the danger of rumour and suspicion without evidence, but the reports on the trial made it clear that the uncommon situation regarding sex and marital infidelity was at the heart of the case. *The Times* reported:

> It was suggested that this was a case of what was called the eternal triangle, but there was one element that was usually found in such cases that was missing here. They had a husband who did not seem to mind what was happening, who knew his wife was going out with Parsons for the whole day, and who had been with him as his wife on two or three occasions, and yet he allowed him to stay in that house ...

This was planted in the jury's mind, and when it came to evidence that Charlotte had tired of Frederick and she wanted to have Parsons all the time. Under questioning, she tried to argue that Parsons had pressured her to leave with him, saying, 'He wanted me to leave my husband. He wanted me to go away with him.'

The summing up by MacKinnon was about the key questions of first, was the victim poisoned with arsenic, and did his wife administer it. The jury was out for an hour and then returned a verdict of guilty. All she said before sentence was passed was, 'I am not guilty.' There was an appeal on 29 June at which Lord Hewart, the Lord Chief Justice, presided. There had been certain weaknesses in the case against her: there was no real evidence that she had bought the poison, and there was no totally certain evidence that she had actually poisoned the food. The evidence was circumstantial, but that was often enough in such cases.

However, before Lord Hewart, the defence made the understandable gambit of bringing in an expert witness to try to counteract Roche Lynch's statements about the location and quantity of the arsenic found. The man in question was Professor William Bone of the Imperial College of Science and Technology. Again, the debate surrounded the issue of the tin. Bone's case was summarized in the appeal court report:

> Dr Roche Lynch's evidence was that 149.6 parts of arsenic per million . . . was so excessive that arsenic must have been burnt in the fire to produce it. The evidence of Professor Bone, which he asked leave to call, would be to the effect that, while the figure varied considerably with different coals, the average normal residue contained in the neighbourhood of 1,100 parts of arsenic per million, and that the lowest normal proportion was about 240 parts per million.

Hewart was not moved. His dismissal was succinct and dogmatic:

> The court is unanimously of the opinion that there is no occasion for the further evidence. The application is of the objectionable kind which we foresaw in a recent case when in very exceptional circumstances we admitted further medical evidence. This kind of possibility was adumbrated and we set our faces like a flint against it . . .

The final words were that there was nothing to the appeal, except that it arose out of a case of murder, and the appeal was dismissed. Charlotte Bryant was hanged on 15 July 1936 at Exeter, by Thomas Pierrepoint. Her last act before death was to write a letter to the King, begging for the Royal pardon. That letter never reached the King, being taken by the Home Secretary. She refused to see her children, and the plight of the family provides a coda to the story.

That is to note that Mrs Violet van der Elst, a noted anti-capital punishment campaigner, drove up to the Exeter prison at eight o'clock and broke through a police cordon. She was arrested and taken before a magistrate, then fined £5. She had aimed to arrive at the moment of execution, but in fact, Charlotte had been hanged at seven o'clock, because of the demonstration outside. Mrs van der Elst started a fund, with a huge first contribution of £50,000 (£1,849,000 today), to help the children of executed convicts. She told the press that she intended to take care of the Bryant children, planning to pay for their education.

Mrs van der Elst was something of an eccentric, but her philanthropy extended to the plight of the condemned person: she joined in all kinds of campaigns and set out to run a media campaign, including having her large saloon car placed in obstructive places around prison, speaking to the assembled crowds, and generally becoming a nuisance.

Is there any possibility that this was a case of an unsafe conviction leading to a wrongful execution? It is not difficult to argue that the forensic evidence was flawed, but then circumstantial evidence had been accepted in hundreds of other similar cases; what makes this more horrific is the mix of morality and legal procedure that provided a guilty verdict.

CHAPTER 6

The Wife Pulled the Trigger

O beware my Lord, of jealousy
It is the green-eyed monster
*   which doth mock*
The meat it feeds on.

Shakespeare, *Othello*

The steel town of Scunthorpe had its problems with crime in the 1930s, along with every other place in which there was immigrant labour, poverty and social divisions of the rich and the poor. But in 1937 the big news in the town was of a killing in a quiet street just a few hundred yards away from the police court. But this was no death during a robbery and no mugging. Just after Christmas 1936 Mrs Doris Teesdale shot her husband with a gun that he kept under a mattress.

Cecil Teasdale was a butcher, twenty-nine years old, and Doris just a year younger. Cecil liked to stay out late and he enjoyed the company of other women. There had been stresses and strains in the marriage for some time and, to make things worse, their first son, just four years old, had died not long before. On the fateful morning, Cecil came down to eat his breakfast and then a maid heard the conversation. The husband saw Doris with the gun and told her to stop fooling. 'I'm not fooling,' she said. Then a shot was fired and Doris ran out in a panic, screaming for help. A doctor was called and a neighbour came to try to help. Cecil was not dead, but severely wounded.

Everything in their story points to a tragic accident and so the court decided, but it was a close-run thing. Doris was sure that the gun only had blanks, and her husband had told her so not long before. In court, Doris Teasdale had to prove that she had no intention of killing her husband, but that she was intending only to frighten him. At the trial in Lincoln, the famous

Mr Justice Travers Humphreys presided, and he put his finger on the legal dilemma: 'If this is the truth it is highly dangerous and most unlawful for any person to fire a revolver in the neighbourhood of another person.' In court, then, lawyers had to probe her real feelings towards her husband, who had taken several days to die in hospital. Mr Richard O'Sullivan prosecuted, and he moved in with the relevant questions, asking if she were 'reckless in this matter if the gun were loaded'. She had taken a gun she knew to be loaded, but that she was convinced there were blanks in it. She said that she was 'fooling' not in the sense of taking the gun to him but in picking it up at all.

The famous Norman Birkett defended, and he drew out her feelings with care and directness:

> Birkett: 'When you married your husband you were very much in love with him?'
> Witness: 'Very deeply.'
> Birkett: 'Did that love for your husband never die?'
> Witness: 'Never.'
> Birkett: 'When you found that he was with other women, staying out ... why didn't you leave him?'
> Witness: 'Because I loved him too much for that.'

When their child had died, Cecil had been out until two in the morning. As Birkett said, 'It was during the week that he lay dying.'

Doris told the court that she went towards the room that morning with the thought of just scaring her husband.

But she stood there and brandished the weapon. When he saw her he had said, 'Stop fooling Dot' and then, 'Oh well, it doesn't matter. It's loaded with blanks.' But before a shot was fired they talked in an animated way about where he had been and why he stayed out. She tried reasoning with him, and she told Birkett that she had never become enraged at the time.

So we have a situation in which a person entered a room carrying a gun with the intention of causing fear, not causing grievous bodily harm and certainly not murder. But it was a tough job sorting out why both murder and manslaughter should be discounted.

They had had a second child, born just over a year before
these events, having married in 1927 in Lincoln; they were
happy until, around 1932, Mr Teasdale took a new shop.
Things became notably unsteady and sometimes rocky. There
were testimonies about their having quarrels – something Doris
denied. 'They were more arguments than quarrels' she said.

But through the eyes of the law, the delicacy of the situation
was summed up by Humphreys: 'The law of this country is
jealous of the lives of its citizens, so jealous that to take the life of
another citizen done without consent of that citizen is murder
... or to take a life by negligently firing a gun which turns out to
be loaded is at least manslaughter.'

On the face of things, it must have seemed as though manslaughter was a strong possibility. After all, what she did could
easily be interpreted as 'reckless' and of course she took the gun
with 'negligence' as to the real facts of the case. What turned
matters in her favour was evidence that Mr Teasdale, not long
before, had fired a chamber, saying that there were merely
blanks there, and then being astonished when a bullet was fired.

O'Sullivan puts things boldly: 'My submission is that she is at
least guilty of manslaughter ...' But as the truth of their lives
together came through, sympathy was gathered for Mrs Doris
Teasdale, partly through the bereavement she had suffered,
and for the stoical way she dealt with the adultery. But mostly,
her ignorance of firearms was obvious and all the witnesses
testifying to words she spoke immediately after the shooting
confirmed this. They also confirmed the view that she was
genuinely shocked at what had happened. The gun, clearly fired
with the intention of firing a blank well wide of the man, had
juddered and he had been hit. He died of peritonitis; the bullet
had broken a rib and entered the abdomen, and then the
peritonitis set in.

Because Teasdale was often out for so long and he tended
to leave the garage doors open, he kept a gun to scare any
intruders. That was reckless, of course. So some of his habits
tended to add to the opinion of Doris as a hapless victim of
his lifestyle and odd ways that developed in court. Not only did
she have a young child and had been a long-suffering wife,
she had also, it was said, been cruelly treated in custody. Her

lawyer had found her in a pitiful state in the police cell, as the local newspaper reported: 'Mr Lewes wished to make a strong protest against the accommodation provided at Scunthorpe for a woman on remand ...'

The sympathy piled up: the human story came through, a tale of tragic proportions and without doubt the tale of a long-suffering women whose actions on that day had been thoughtless and foolish rather than malevolent.

By 16 January, the townspeople of Scunthorpe had raised a defence fund for Doris Teasdale amounting to £350, a very large sum (worth almost £13,000 today). She was on remand at Hull prison at the time, and a local butcher, Tom Fisher, after consulting Mr T J Lewis, her solicitor, had taken charge of that fund-raising. He did a great job, even announcing the campaign on local cinema screens. It was known that she had no money and a good 'brief' was desired for her. She got the very best: Norman Birkett KC.

In the biography of Birkett by Montgomery Hyde, it is noted that Birkett's opinion was reiterated: he had said, 'When you are dealing with the important question of intent, consider her attitude in the [witness] box. There was no venom. It was plain she never intended to do the slightest harm to her husband. The atmosphere of that room was not threatening ...'

Doris Teasdale stood in the dock on 12 February 1937, a frail, pathetic figure. It was noted that she stood 'pale but composed' between two women warders.

Mr Justice Humphreys took over an hour to sum up; he was confident that the jury should settle on the decision of manslaughter. That would, of course, have been expected after such a direction from his eminence.

But those present were in for a surprise, as it was reported at the time:

> The jury, absent for two hours and ten minutes, disagreed and to the relief and astonishment of an eagerly awaiting court, they returned a verdict of not guilty on both charges.

The young woman 'sobbed for an hour' in between thanking her legal team. After that she disappeared into the rural calm of Lincolnshire, 'reunited with her sixteen-month-old baby'. As for Cecil Walter Teasdale, he was buried at Brumby Cemetery, Scunthorpe. He had died in Scunthorpe War Memorial Hospital. Some say the truth was buried with him, others are convinced that the legal outcome was the right one. The house still stands – just a small house in a quiet street near the town centre.

CHAPTER 7

The Mystery of Walter Rowland

I wish to say that the statements I have given confessing to a murder are absolutely untrue.

David Ware

This is a story with a potentially tragic undertone, a case with twists and turns, strange coincidences and faulty police work. First, it is necessary to give the salient facts, and then the assessment of the problematic case may be made.

In 1934, this 'minder' from Derbyshire was sentenced to death after he killed his two-year-old daughter by strangling her with a stocking. In his appeal statement, Rowland had said, 'I am innocent and a victim of circumstances.' In short, the prosecution, it was felt at appeal, never really proved the crime, but that there was enough to persuade the jury of Rowland's guilt. The evidence was seen as purely circumstantial. In the summing up, the judge said, 'It is perfectly clear that the little child has been killed by somebody, that she had been left in the charge of her father ... and she was murdered while her mother was elsewhere ...'

The appeal was dismissed, but Rowland was later reprieved. He served some time and then joined the armed forces. Like Simcox, though, years later, he was once again on a murder charge. This time the scene was Manchester, and the body of prostitute Olive Balchin was found on waste ground in Cumberland Street, Manchester. She had been battered to death with hammer blows to the head. But Rowland was a violent man, and had another conviction as well as the child-murder. He was in Manchester, so he was questioned; he had an alibi, stating that he was at 36 Hyde Road, in lodgings. In fact his presence had been noted, and he had been signed in on the night of the murder, but that was overlooked. But Rowland admitted that he had been with Olive. He also made several rash statements to the police, including the fact that he had VD and that if it had been Olive who had given him that then she deserved what she got.

Everything was pointing to him as the killer. He was identified on parades, and the times of his stated movements meant that it was just possible for him to have been with Olive at the time she died. He was charged and forensic evidence made his situation look very bleak, notably the fact that in his trouser turn-ups there was a cluster of materials that matched the same substances at the bomb-site. He was sentenced to death, but then came the stunning news that a man in Walton gaol had confessed to the crime. This was David Ware, and he wrote: 'I wish to confess that I killed Olive Balshaw [that spelling is important] with a hammer at the bombed site in Deansgate, Manchester, on Saturday 19 October at about 10.00pm. We had been in a picture house near the Belle Vue stadium.'

This was to prove tantalisingly ambiguous and problematic for the detectives who went to check the man out. The dapper and celebrated Detective Inspector Herbert Hannam of Scotland Yard led the interrogation. Amazingly, Ware gave a detailed account of the night at the pictures, with lots of other details that seemed convincing. Surely this would mean that, like Simcox in 1914, Rowland was going to be saved from the noose a second time? But Hannam was of the opinion that the details Ware had mentioned could be seen by someone passing by – he did not accept the tale as convincing and thought that Ware was fantasising – being of unsound mind. A report was written for the Home Secretary on Ware's statement. He said his confession was a fabrication: 'I do remember reading in the paper about the peculiarity of the buttons on the coat worn by the murdered woman.' He also finally said, 'I would like to say I am sorry I have given the trouble I have and I didn't realise the serious consequences it might entail had the confession been believed.'

Herbert Hannam reported that he had found a number of press cuttings with details relevant to the case. He wrote: 'In two of these cuttings the victim is said to be 'Balshaw.' In one of these cuttings published within a few days of the discovery of the body the name is said to be Balshaw ...'

Was Rowland innocent after all? The questions began very early in the post-execution history of the case.

Leslie Hale thought so. In his book, *Hanged in Error* (1961), he says, 'The register at the lodging house where Ware claimed to have spent the Saturday night from about 11.15pm onwards had been inspected by two police officers after Ware's confession ... Inspector Hannam went to see it in late February. He was told that the book had been destroyed. The report does not state whether an explanation was asked for or supplied.'

Now we return to the murder itself and look in more detail. The story began on a Sunday – 26 October 1946. It was peaceful, and that must have been welcomed after the Blitz. The bombings had left Manchester, along with many other great cities, a place of desolate bomb-sites, natural adventure playgrounds for children. On that day, two boys went from a service at St Mary's church into Deansgate; passing a bomb site, they saw the usual crumbling stone and the scattered vegetation. But they also saw a corpse. They ran to it, then stopped to stare in awe. The body was that of a woman, with her arms out and her legs bent underneath her body. She was wearing an overcoat and a beret, and near her was a handbag. Naturally, the boys sprinted to find a policeman.

Detectives Valentine and Stainton came to the crime scene and saw at once that here was someone who had been beaten to death: it was the standard 'blunt object' killing. In fact, it didn't take Sherlock Holmes to see that the murder weapon was lying just a few feet away – a hammer, still with flesh and blood smeared on it. There were signs of a struggle, and in the handbag they found what everyone had at that time – an Identity Card. The victim was Olive Balchin.

The next stage was for the doctor to take a look, and a police surgeon came, along with DS William Page. The investigation swung into action, and the first place to go and ask questions was in Birmingham, where Olive lived, the address on her Card. Her home was found, a lodging house, and the landlady described Olive as having a sad face. That was her basic description. How was the detective to know? He had only seen a corpse, but it was a personality trait, and that counts for something in a murder investigation. The victim had last been seen in Birmingham two days earlier.

Following up on that lead, the police learned that there was a couple who had brought Olive up, as she was an orphan. The foster-father said that as Olive had grown up, she had not been happy, and that there had been a miserable affair that did not work out. When she moved away, her name changed from Balchin to Balshaw, as if she was determined to start a new life. But that new life was destined to be prostitution.

The police did not immediately know that. They concentrated on the usual gambits: the forensic report stated that the death was indeed caused by the hammer, a very distinctive one known as a leather-beater's hammer. The obvious move then was to find out where such a tool would be sold, and sure enough, the owner of a toolshop in Downing Street recalled selling it. It was marked, so he knew the tool exactly, and the man who had bought it was described: 'He was a rather handsome man, medium build, well-dressed, and he had a kind of low, rich voice. I think he was wearing a tan coat and a grey slouch hat.' That was an incredibly precise and useful visual description, and it helped enormously in the hunt. The hammer had been sold on Saturday afternoon. Sales of that particular tool were so rare that the shopkeeper recalled the sale vividly. In fact, the description was so specific that a waitress at a café in Deansgate, when given the words, immediately said that she recalled a woman fitting Olive's description being with a man wearing those clothes, and that had been late on the Saturday night.

The pieces of the jigsaw were fitting together very easily. The couple were also seen by a publican very late on that night, standing at the edge of the bombsite. He heard enough to know that they had been quarrelling. The police had dressed a WPC as Olive in order to circulate to find other witnesses, and shown the picture, the publican confirmed that that was the woman he saw.

What was then needed was hard evidence from the scientists in forensics. But unfortunately, there were no prints on the hammer, and no shoeprints on the site earth either. Then the unexpected happened. The waitress in the café, when talking again to a detective, stopped and pointed at a man sitting at a table and said, 'That's him!' The man was immediately questioned: he was Walter Rowland, and he had recently been demobbed, and was lodging in Furness Street. He was a Derbyshire man but had come to Manchester looking for work. He was born in New Mills, and when the detectives were told that yes, he did know Olive, and had spent time with her, the case must have seemed sorted. But Rowland said on the Saturday night he had had a drink with the woman in the past, but on the Saturday in question had caught a bus to New Mills to see his mother and then returned to his lodgings. The times of the bus and the journey were assessed, and the detectives saw that there was a 'window' – there would have been time for Rowland to go to the café and then kill Olive.

It looked black for Rowland, who was strongly insisting on this being a case of mistaken identity, because both the waitress and the publican picked out Rowland and identified him. The witness who could give him an alibi was the landlord of the hostel. He said he could confirm that Rowland had stayed at his place on that night, but when pressed to say he was absolutely sure, he could not say so. The alibi could not be confirmed. Again, the next stage was up to the forensics team, who were studying things more deeply and thoroughly at that point.

The most important aspects of the information given by witnesses were confirmed by the forensic analysis: hairs were found on Rowland's overcoat, and he admitted that he had worn that coat on the evening of the murder. In his trouser turn-ups brick dust was found, along with a number of other residues which were all evident on the bomb site, such as charcoal and leaf remains. There were bloodstains on one of his shoes, although these could not be confirmed as having belonged to Olive. All the material evidence pointed to Rowland as the killer and he was charged with murder.

In court, at Manchester Assizes, right next to Strangeways prison, Mr Justice Sellers presided and for the Crown, Basil Nield acted. The heart of any argument was motive, of course. Why did he kill Olive? The reasoning was the oldest in history – the spurned lover. Nield argued that Rowland had wanted to marry Olive but had been turned down. The narrative of the crime he presented concerned the visit to his mother, the return to town to meet Olive, followed by the argument, and then the attack.

Kenneth Burke spoke for the defence and Rowland insisted he was not guilty, repeating what he had told police time and time again: that he was peacefully asleep in the hostel when the murder took place. He was, he said, not the man the witnesses thought they had seen. Defence argued that the evidence was simply circumstantial. Burke's main line of thought was given to the jury: 'Does this constitute evidence of murder? The man who killed Miss Balchin with this weapon must have held it firmly while striking the blows. Yet the prosecution has failed to prove that there were any fingerprints upon it.' That was a solid argument, but of course, the killer could have been wearing gloves. Even the blood on the shoe was not definitely from the victim. Burke did a convincing job of casting doubt on the prosecution's case, and he closed with some high drama, saying, 'Can you send a man to his death on the basis of this evidence?'

After two hours, the jury returned with a guilty verdict. Rowland was galvanised into action, saying vehemently that he was not guilty and that they had condemned an innocent man. He said, 'Somewhere there is a person who knows I stand here an innocent man.' The judge put on the black cap and the death sentence was passed.

The process towards an appeal went on, but then came the shock of a confessional letter, written apparently from St Helens. Detectives went to work to try and trace the author. On 24 January, after a man in Walton jail, Liverpool, David Ware, told the prison authorities: 'I killed the Balchin woman. I wrote those letters.' Ware was interviewed and notes taken. His facts tallied remarkably well with known events, and most telling of all was a reference to going to the pictures – something Rowland had told the police. This confession happened just as the appeal was about to take place; Lord Goddard, who was to sit there, ordered an adjournment.

This is the point at which Inspector Hannam of the Yard makes his entrance. Ware's statements had been convincing, so verification was needed as to whether or not he really was the killer. In one statement, for instance, he had written:

After meeting the woman at the Hippodrome Theatre, we got on a tramcar the indicator of which read Belle Vue. We left the tramcar at the stadium then walked up the road quite a long way until we came to a third-rate picture house together . . .

and also:

After I had felt this woman feeling in my pockets, I felt in my trousers cash pocket and found that a ten shilling note which I was certain I had, was gone . . .

This kind of detail was very impressive. A ten shilling note had indeed been found on Olive's person.

There was an enquiry conducted into the confession, led by John Jolly, and from this we learn what Hannam did. Jolly sent Hannam to dig deeper into Ware, and the result was this statement from the 'Count of Scotland Yard':

I have examined numerous press cuttings published prior to the committal of Rowland. One of these includes . . . a photograph of the coat worn by Balchin and comment is made of the distinctive nature of the buttons upon that coat. In at least two of these reports the price paid for the hammer is quoted . . . In two of these press cuttings which appeared quite early after the discovery of the body the name of the victim is said to be 'Balshaw' . . .

Ware had, Hannam argued, read all the press reports closely, and that is why he had created a plausible narrative of the supposed time he spent with Olive. Crucially, the name Balshaw rather than Balchin was given: in the papers she was Balshaw.

The appeal finally took place on 27 January. Justices Humphries and Lewis presided, and they heard Burke put forward material relating to Ware, but in the end, Humphreys concluded:

The court has come to the conclusion that this appeal must be dismissed; but as a question has arisen here with regard to an application to cal the evidence of a witness who is alleged to have made some confession with regard to this crime, and the court has refused to allow that evidence to be given . . .

He was to hang and there was no hope. Henry Cecil, in the first book written on the case, insists that a major factor in the death sentence was that Rowland was 'a dog with a bad name'. Back in 1927 he had been convicted of grievous bodily harm after trying to strangle May Schofield, and despite this they married, and in 1932 he had strangled and killed their child Mavis. Later, he had twice tried to take his own life.

Rowland was hanged on 27 February 1947 at Manchester. The hangman was Albert Pierrepoint, fresh from Germany where he had been hanging Nazis. In contrast, the topping of just another seedy woman-killer was bread and butter work. He makes no mention of it in his memoirs.

The doubt in this case, and the lingering worry that an innocent man died, hinges partly on the nature of Ware's letters, but partly on certain mysteries, the most notable of which is that reported by Leslie Hale in 1961:

> The register at the lodging house where Ware claimed to have spent the night from about 11.15 onwards, had been inspected by two policemen after Ware's confession, late in January. Inspector Hannam went to inspect it late in February. He was told that the book had been destroyed. The report does not disclose whether any information was asked for or supplied.

But there is a strange coda to this story: on 10 July 1951, David Ware tried to kill a woman in Bristol. He had bought a hammer and had tried to batter her to death. Ware told police, 'I have killed a woman. I don't know what is the matter with me. I keep on having an urge to hit women on the head.' He was found guilty but did not hang, for reasons of unsound mind. In fact, he took his own life in Broadmoor, hanging himself in his cell in 1954.

CHAPTER 8

Buck Ruxton

Red stains on the carpet,
Red stains on the knife,
Oh Dr Buck Ruxton
You murdered your wife ...

Adaptation of the popular song
Red Sails in the Sunset

This is a story of maggots, old newspapers and sharp knives. That might seem to be a bizarre statement, but in fact these are the key words in one of the most remarkable stories of amoral, brutal and savage murders ever carried out in England. It brought the very specialised science of forensic entomology into the public domain, so that readers of the morning papers, once they went past the revulsion of reading about chopped up bodies, had to try to understand how blow flies – the bluebottles they swatted every day with rolled-up newspaper – helped in the investigation of the killing of two women.

The story begins at a stream near Moffat in Dumfriesshire on 19 September 1935. It is a pleasant spot, and has always been popular with holidaymakers in search of tranquillity. But when Susan Johnson walked to a bridge to look down at the stream she saw something protruding from a package of some kind. Taking a closer look, she almost retched: the object was a human arm. Susan ran to her brother, and he went to inspect the 'package'. It was an arm, wrapped in old newspapers. In no time, the place was full of police.

Later that day, a sergeant from the Dumfriesshire Constabulary found more packages containing various chunks of corpses. The search was on, as the wider area around the Linn (the stream) was searched in the following weeks. There was even a piece of body – a foot – found on the road, nine miles away from Moffat. It was not until 4 November that the last find was discovered, a hand and forearm. In total, the pieces of human corpses included two heads, seventeen chunks of arms and legs, and lots of smaller pieces of flesh. They would have to be inspected for whatever information they had which might help the police, so the body parts were sent to Edinburgh University. That is where the maggots took centre stage in the enquiry.

Meanwhile the usual police moves were made: searches for missing persons, checks on motorists who had used the road, and of course hunts for possible witnesses who might have seen anything unusual around the Linn. The first breakthrough came with the realisation that one of the newspapers used to wrap some of the remains was a special local edition of the *Sunday Graphic*, only distributed around Morecambe and Lancaster. The next logical step was to check in those two towns for anyone who had been reported missing.

Mary Jane Rogerson was working as a maid in the home of Dr Buck Ruxton, who had his practice in Lancaster, and her parents were becoming very worried about her by the 20 September. She had not been seen for five days and that was very unusual for her: Mary always kept in touch with her parents. They were at first mollified by Ruxton but eventually went to the police. At the same time, a Glasgow detective called Ewing had been extremely observant and attentive to all sources of information; he read in another paper that the wife of Dr Ruxton was missing, and then he saw the similarity between the description given in the news of Mary Rogerson and the account given of some of the remains at Moffat, given by the forensics expert in Edinburgh, Dr Glaister.

Things were falling into place, and the focus of interest was Ruxton. When Mrs Rogerson identified items of clothing from the parcels of limbs, she was sure that Mary was one of the deceased: specifically, a patch sewn on a blouse and some rompers made her sure that they belonged to her daughter. The Ruxtons used to go to a Mrs Holme in Grange-over-Sands, across Morecambe Bay, to collect clothes, and a visit to that lady in the quiet seaside village confirmed what Mrs Rogerson had surmised. Fine details were noticed, such as a specific knot tied in the elastic of the rompers which Ms Holme saw at once.

Enquiries were made about Ruxton. Obviously, not only did the objects related to the case point to him, but also the fact that the skill needed to cut up the bodies in such professional ways made it certain that the person who had done this had medical knowledge.

Who was Buck Ruxton? He was born Bukhtyar Hakim, in 1899, and was from a Parsee family: these are people who are descended from Persians (Persia is the former name of Iran). They moved to Gujarat in India in the seventeenth century to escape religious persecution, and in the process of historical change, they were active in creating the city of Bombay, and they were a solid base of the middle class in that place. The Hakims were of that kind. Hakim qualified in medicine in Bombay, and also became a surgeon. He won first class honours in midwifery and gynaecology, and he married a Parsee woman when he was twenty-six. But that did not work out, and he went to Britain.

That was the beginning of a new life and a new identity for him. He was now Dr Gabriel Hakim. It was entirely natural that a medical man would move to Edinburgh – one of the most highly-respected centres of medical study in Europe. There he was not so brilliant, failing to achieve a Fellowship of the College of Surgeons, but his Indian qualifications were enough for him to go into practice. He married a second time, his new wife was Dutch – Isabella van Ess. As he took on aspects of a new life, the Indian heritage was played down. He changed his name by deed poll. Thus Dr Buck Ruxton came into being, establishing his practice in Lancaster. In the early 1930s they had children and at that point they employed Mary.

On 14 September, Isabella went to Blackpool to be with her sister, a Mrs Nelson, who was on holiday there from Edinburgh. For some time, Ruxton had been insanely jealous of his wife, always suspecting that she was having affairs. On that occasion, he thought she had been to Blackpool to meet a man, and when she came back, he was waiting for her, and in a rage. He attacked her, strangled her and she was stabbed. Mary was working close by and came to see what was happening. That was her death warrant. She could not be allowed to live and so she too was killed, also strangled. We know from Chief

Constable Vann, who led the investigation, what happened next:

> He dragged the bodies to the bathroom, laid them on a long seat approximately 15 feet long and 18 inches wide, and cut them up. After filling the bath with cold water, as each limb was dismembered he cut the arteries and placed it in the bath, thereby allowing the blood to dissolve. Having drained the portions of bodies completely of blood he dried them with cotton wool, wrapped them in sheets and newspapers and packed them into suitable parcels ...

He must have driven to Moffat through the night and then returned home early. He was heard by his charwoman going to and from a room in the house in the middle hours of the day of the 19 September. He was, police were sure, shifting the bodies and storing them in a large cupboard. When the body parts were bagged up, there was a clear attempt to confound matters by mixing them – so that for instance, his wife's pelvis was packed with Mary's legs.

Ruxton was not the main focus in another sense. Basic police work leading to him from the clothes and the newspaper were one thing, but the forensic experts were needed to make matters regarding the identity of the victims certain. What was needed was a reconstruction of the remains, and the man with that unenviable task was Professor John Brash from Edinburgh, but he had Professor Glaister to help, and the latter became the main forensic witness at the trial. First, the parts were assigned to the labels of 'Body No. 1' and 'Body No. 2'. Chief Constable Vann, writing in 1937, listed these:

Body No. 1	Body No. 2
Two arms	Two arms
Two forearms and hands	Two forearms
Two thighs	Two hands, minus fingers
Two legs	Two thighs
Two feet	Two legs
No trunk	One foot
	Complete trunk

The softer parts of the remains were covered by maggots. Dr A G Mearns was able to gauge the time the murders took place from the state of the maggots. The source of the maggots is that they are the pupae of blow flies, insects attracted to rotting flesh. Specimens are studied to ascertain how long ago the female flies settled on the body and laid eggs – usually done at the orifices of the body. The flies have four life stages, and so that helps timing to take place, as each stage exists for an average period of time, as long as the temperature has been right.

The cause of death in both cases was strangulation, and it was also found that, after study of the top of the stairs, the killings had taken place there. After the main part of the forensic work, the time and place of death was known. The main task was to reconstruct the bodies as far as possible. The two bodies were assembled as much as could be done; there was no problem in defining the sex; pieces of flesh were found to be female breasts. From skull, bones and teeth the relative ages of the two women were ascertained. The result of all this was that Body 1 was between eighteen and twenty-five years old and just under 5 feet; Body 2 was between thirty-five and forty-five years old and was about 5 feet 3 inches.

Yet another expert played a part too: Dr Arthur Hutchinson studied the teeth. He could assess the dates of the extraction of teeth from sockets and gums. Some teeth had been removed just before the dissections, while others were long-standing.

By all these means, a narrative was put together, a forensic story to back up whatever the police could get out of Ruxton himself. In fact, that was to prove a very simple thing to do. As Chief Constable Vann recalled:

I asked him to come over to my office on Saturday, 12 October, 1935, as the police had some information about his wife . . . he was taken aback to find a number of highly placed police officials there. I told him I was anxious to trace his wife and maid and suggested that he might be able to give some assistance in finding them. He was also asked to account for his movements from the night of 14 September to 29 September. He was cautioned . . . Ruxton appeared to be delighted to have the opportunity and said, 'Go on, ask me . . . ask me anything you like, I will be only too pleased to tell you . . .'

Vann and others fired the important questions at him, and the police officer recalled that after being charged with the murder, Ruxton was 'in turn violent and emotional and on one occasion thumped violently on the table . . .' But a little later he was apologetic and repented his lack of self-control.

The trial was at Manchester High Court of Justice on 2 March 1936. Mr Justice Singleton presided. Ruxton was defended by the great Norman Birkett and the prosecution was led by J C Jackson and Maxwell Fyfe. Before that, back in November 1935, when he first appeared before the magistrates, he had been loud and violent, asking crazy questions and raving. Of course he had been the biggest story in the media for the months preceding the trial. Although the trial took eleven days, the outcome was certain really, such was the evidence. There were no witnesses other than Ruxton himself for the defence, and as well as the forensic evidence, there was all the evidence from the scene, notably the clumsy attempts made to burn the carpet and other materials on which blood had been left.

Norman Birkett, who later became Lord Justice, had been prominent in a number of major criminal cases in the previous years, but this was a challenge to say the least. As his biographer, H Montgomery Hyde, explained, 'There were over 200 exhibits in court, including a scale model of the prisoner's house complete with furnishings and the nameplate on the door.' Ruxton added further pressure on Birkett by constantly scribbling notes, suggesting questions he should ask.

It took seven days for the prosecution to present all their evidence and give their arguments. One of the most remarkable aspects of the forensic evidence was that of the photographic work done by Professor Brash. He had two photos of the women enlarged to life-size proportions; he then photographed the two skulls, making these images equate to the picture of the women as she was in life. The distinct facial features were then transferred to sheets of transparent paper, and then the photographers produced positive and negative images which could be superimposed. When seen by a jury, this was so convincing as proof of the body being that of Isabella, that it was a keystone in the case for the Crown. Birkett tried to think of a way to make this inadmissible but failed.

Birkett wrote notes on the structure of the defence, the most important of these being:

> The medical evidence to be of any avail must deny the medical evidence of the prosecution in its essential feature, i.e. these are the bodies of Mrs Ruxton and Mary Rogerson, and I am informed by medical experts that this is impossible. Contradictions in minor matters are useless . . . In my clear and very strong view, if Dr Ruxton desires to give evidence, we should confine our evidence to him . . .

In the dock, Ruxton's mental state was more than evident. He said, after dabbing his tearful eyes with a handkerchief, 'We could not live with each other and we could not live without each other . . . He who loves most chastises most . . .' He denied any acts of violence and tried to explain away the blood and the petrol (found around the place and used to try to burn the carpet).

When the prosecution tackled the subject of his wife's supposed infidelity, this exchange took place:

> Question: 'You have for a considerable time thought your wife unfaithful?'
>
> Reply: 'She has done some silly things that would not have been done by a sensible woman . . .'

He explained that by infidelity, Ruxton meant 'not a misconduct of a sexual nature but a transfer of affection . . .'

It was inevitable that Ruxton would be found guilty, and he was. Sentence of death was given. Even in his last words before judgement, Ruxton was verbose, scatty and odd, saying,

> Subject to the point that I be allowed to appeal . . . in the administration of justice . . . I submit to your Lordship . . . I want to thank everybody for the patience and fairness at my trial . . .

There was an appeal. All Birkett could do was concentrate on the fact that Ruxton's car was very clean. He said, 'There was not a spot of blood on the car, isn't that a most remarkable thing?' If there was doubt on Ruxton's long drive to Moffat, then in spite of all the forensic evidence, the prosecution's case might collapse. But Lord Hewart's decision was stated directly,

completely reliant on the forensic analysis: 'The evidence that
the dismembered bodies were those of Mrs Ruxton and Mary
Rogerson is really overwhelming . . . The application is of a kind
that the court cannot grant.'

Ruxton was hanged on 12 May 1936 at Manchester. But
before he died he wrote to Birkett to ask him to help his three
children: 'I am leaving three bonnie little mites behind. If you
can, please be good to them . . .' Birkett was good to them. He
arranged for them to be brought up, placed in an orphanage.
But a stranger thing then happened. Ruxton wrote another
letter, a confession, and he handed it to a journalist:

> I killed Mrs Ruxton in a fit of temper because I thought she
> had been with a man. I was mad at the time. Mary Rogerson
> was present at the time. I had to kill her.
>   B Ruxton

As Montgomery Hyde pointed out, 'This sealed confession
was unique, since never before, so far as is known, had a document of this character been entrusted to a newspaper by a man
who was destined for the scaffold.'

Ruxton was paid the then huge sum of £3,000 (almost
£111,000 in today's money) for that confession – money which
easily paid Birkett's fees.

We know a great deal about Buck Ruxton, but what still
remains in doubt is who hanged him. According to John
Eddleston, in his massive encyclopaedia of the hanged of the last
century, the hangman is unknown. Yet Steve Fielding, also a
specialist historian of the gallows, says that Ruxton was hanged
by Tom Pierrepoint, assisted by Robert Wilson. Fielding notes
that in Pierrepoint's diary, the name of Ruxton is written:
'Parsee doctor Buck Ruxton . . . was the next name in Tom's
diary.' That would seem to settle the issue.

CHAPTER 9

The Wallace Enigma

Misleading telephone messages, false addresses, contrived alibis, numerous witnesses, deep-seated family secrets – this case has them all ...

Clifford Elmer

Some crimes defy explanation. Some crimes have an abundance of facts and fine detail, yet still offer no resolution, no closure. The reasons for this may be because too much time has passed and history has cast a dark shadow over events and motives. Yet the enigma may be from some other reason, something to do with failures of logic and apparent deceptions. If the narrative of a crime is such that all the resources of a mind such as that of Sherlock Holmes would find defeat the only outcome, then the events will go on and on, being revisited by the most assiduous and enquiring minds of writers, criminologists and novelists.

If a search were to be made to find the crime that best fits this description, it would very likely be that of the murder of Mrs Wallace. This is a murder story. A life was definitely taken. But the journey towards a solution is a succession of dead ends. In an ordinary suburb of an English city, someone took a life and in a brutal way. At the moment, the identity of the killer is shrouded in a mist of uncertainty. One candidate has always been under scrutiny – her husband, William. But again, certainty eludes investigation.

If Liverpool can claim to be the setting for several infamous and problematic homicides, then first among these has to be the Wallace case. The year 1931 was notable for its crime mysteries. There was the notorious 'Blazing Car' case in Northumberland, still unsolved, and also the Margaret Schofield case in Dewsbury (unsolved). But in sheer complexity, the death that has been called by many 'the perfect murder' is Liverpool's own, and presents the historian with a riddle: if William Wallace, gentle chess-playing insurance agent living in a quiet suburb, did indeed create an alibi and a hoax, then why did he make it all so difficult for himself? There were easier ways to create a ruse and a suspicious stranger.

The story began on 19 January 1931, when a phone call was made to the Central Chess Club in Liverpool by a man calling himself Qualtrough. He wanted to see Wallace urgently, on a business matter. Wallace was not yet at his club, but he was due to arrive to play a match at 7.00pm. Wallace arrived at 7.40pm, and then he was told about the phone call. The club was at the City café, and Wallace had not been doing too well of late, walking the streets for the Prudential. This call meant a potential customer, so he asked about the address given. Here lies the heart of the mystery: Qualtrough said he lived at Menlove Gardens East – an address that did not exist. Wallace asked several people about the address, and it was known that there was a street called Menlove Gardens North.

All this became important when Wallace's steps are traced the next day, when he went in search of the mystery man. He left his home in Wolverton Street and went to Smithdown Road; then he caught a No 4 tram at Lodge Lane. We know that he went to Menlove Gardens and started looking for 'East' in the area. He made a point of asking lots of people about the address. But by 8.00pm he had given up and went home. It was when he arrived home, just before 9.00pm, that he found the body of his wife. Julia Wallace lay in a pool of her own blood, in her cosy room.

The Wallaces were a quiet couple; neighbours reported no scenes of anger or disagreement. William was a bookish man; he read Marcus Aurelius and based his behaviour and attitudes on that Roman's stoical philosophy. He was firm and controlled right through the coming investigation and trial, something that went surely against him. The image he gave was of a callous, unfeeling man, who should have shown extreme emotion after the violent killing of his wife in their own home. Wallace had been born in the Lake District in 1878; he had worked for a short while in India, and then in Ripon, before settling down to the life of a clerk in Liverpool. He had married Julia in 1913.

We need to ask more questions about William Wallace. In fact, all major studies of the case have tried to assess his character based on what we know of him. A true understanding of the case has to be based on an assessment of his personality. He lived quietly, and his wife was very cultured and refined; she played the piano and took an active interest in the arts. He liked chess, worked hard to practise his stoicism in his everyday life, and also liked to conduct amateur experiments in chemistry, having a small lab in his home. He took up the violin after turning forty. In fact, this profile suggests a man who wanted to be, on his own level and on his own terms, a Renaissance man.

In 1950, the writer F J P Veale provided an interesting assessment of this aspect of Wallace, responding to the cerebral element in the man:

> The murder of his wife gave nationwide publicity to what before had only been known by a narrow circle of acquaintances. William Herbert Wallace was a highbrow, not indeed an academic highbrow, but nevertheless a genuine and persistent highbrow. Far from limiting his intellectual activities like a healthy- minded man of his class to sports results, crossword puzzles and an occasional denunciation of the government in power, Wallace presumed to study and investigate subjects quite outside his humble sphere of life.

In fact, his stoicism went against him. Such a view of life involved suppressing any public show of emotion. This meant that after the killing, it was noticed that his behaviour did not seem to fall in line with expectations about how a bereaved husband in those circumstances should behave.

Wallace was arguably a typical example of the autodidact, the man who is self-taught and who chooses his intellectual and cultural pursuits. He had been a political agent in Ripon earlier in his life and had then worked in India and China in sales, but his health had suffered. Working in insurance suited him admirably: he excelled in keeping records, he was meticulous in everything, and he had a certain level of charm. Clients told police that Wallace told humorous stories and was good company. In other words he had a social self – he projected personality when there was a need to do so. Otherwise he was very reserved.

All this falls in line with the thoughts of Marcus Aurelius, the writer who most influenced his view of life. The essence of Marcus is that he had been a Roman emperor, had participated in life and had known status, but then had withdrawn into the private life so admired in Roman philosophical thinking. A perusal of Marcus's book, *The Meditations*, soon offers an understanding of Wallace. The spirit of that book is that a man should have a regulated life, have dignity, not suffer fools gladly, and learn a broad acceptance of things. For instance, there we have: 'I learned from Sextus ... the example of a family governed in an orderly manner, gravity without affectation, and to tolerate ignorant persons.' Through the book runs a line of thought which perfectly matches Wallace's professional life: 'he had the power to readily accommodate himself to all'. The stress is on how such things as piety and abstinence are learned. Marcus makes much of the need to have 'abstinence not only from evil deeds but from evil thoughts.'

The backbone of stoicism is the notion of perseverance. At one point, Marcus writes: 'I never stop enquiry in all matters of deliberation ... never stop investigation, though being satisfied with appearances.' When Wallace went in search of Menlove Gardens East, he persisted. He went on, in spite of the fact that several people he met had no idea where that address was. Of course, it did not exist. From the viewpoint of the prosecution, the search for Qualtrough was so packed with apparently deliberate conversations with people, including a police officer, that here was a man creating an alibi; but from the viewpoint of the defence, here was an assiduous man following the precepts of his everyday philosophy.

The scene of crime was horrific. When Wallace came home, he could not open the front door, so he went around to the back. He managed to enter, walked upstairs, and found nothing unusual; but when he went down to the parlour and turned on the light, there was her body, lying face down on the rug. There was a pool of blood around her head and such was the force of a blow to her skull that bone was visible. Wallace was accompanied by a friend, Jack Johnson, as he saw this, and Johnson went to bring a police officer.

Meanwhile, Wallace realised that his insurance takings had been stolen from a box in the kitchen. But it was puzzling that a jar of pound notes in the bedroom had not been stolen, despite the fact that they were smudged with blood.

When PC Williams arrived, he and Wallace checked details, but then the forensic expert came, Professor MacFall. He discovered no less than ten more wound marks on the head. There was a mess in the house – evidence of an apparent frenzy. But MacFall noted that the gas-lights were out, so the rage and the supposed search for booty would have taken place in the dark. Also, there were no blood-marks in places where one would have expected them, such as on door handles for instance.

Clearly, Wallace himself would have to be questioned intensively, as there were so many pointers to an alibi and so many oddities at the scene of the murder that did not seem to square with the supposed crazed murder and attack.

DS Hubert Moore led the investigation. He had had long experience, over thirty years of police work. At Dale Street police station, the interviews began. Attention was paid to the Qualtrough call, and to the witnesses who recalled talking to Wallace on his hopeless quest for Menlove Gardens East. It all appeared to be so fabricated, after all: a phone call at a point when there would be an alibi and yet enough time for Wallace to have made the call himself before arriving at the chess club; then all that asking for directions even to the point of making sure that conversations were memorable. It must have all seemed so purposeful to Moore as he faced this quiet, restrained and inscrutable man who controlled his emotions with perfection.

Amazingly, the Qualtrough phone call was traced; it was made from a box defined as Anfield 1627 – a box only 400 yards from Wallace's house in Wolverton Street. But evidence at the scene was unavailable: there was no weapon, no prints and no items found even in the drains and sewers. It was noted, though, that a poker was missing. More important, what would be the motive? Julia had only £20 due from insurance on her life. Wallace had no need of that as he had money saved in his account. At the trial, people started looking for motives in the area of personality and relationship, even to noting Wallace's diary entries, such as one comment about Julia's 'aimless chatter'. But in context, he had written this after her death, saying that he missed her 'loving smiles and aimless chatter'.

The trial began on 22 April at St George's Hall. The judge was Mr Justice Wright; for the prosecution there was E G Hemmerde, and Roland Oliver for the defence. They were all brilliant lawyers in their way: but they were to find several anomalies and unanswered questions in this affair. Wallace's own statement included his own assertion that any hint of him having killed his wife was 'monstrous'. In gathering evidence for the defence (and they had to concentrate on the timing of a milk delivery at the murder house) a certain Elsie Wright, who was sure that the call at the house, at which Julia was alive, was close to a 6.45pm, not 6.30pm. Little details such as this would count for a great deal in the case, as everything rested on the movements of Wallace around Liverpool that day.

Everything except the issue of the raincoat. Wallace's mackintosh was under Julia's body. Here, the limitations of forensics at the time were exposed, particularly in blood movements and splattering, the blood on this coat being either caused by the wounding, or in fact dripping after death. There were also burn stains on the coat, so another question arose: did Wallace fail in an attempt to burn the material? Or equally sensible was the line of thought that it could have been burned in the attack, because Julia was close to the gas fire.

The questioning by the prosecution was aimed at locating all the strange and oddly convenient circumstances of the phone call, the attempt to find the address, and the arguably transparent and feeble creation of an alibi. It had also seemed unconvincing that an innocent man would have walked upstairs in his home before going through to the parlour, the implication being that he was fabricating a likely 'geography' of the movements of the supposed frenzied attacker. Equally, in the examination of Julia Wallace's nature and character, it had been made extremely unlikely that she would have a lover, so if the motive of the anonymous killer was related to a crime of passion, then where was the evidence for that?

So profound has been the study of the case that arguments for and against his guilt tend to be lengthy and complex. But this would be a reasonable summary.

The case for the defence

- The phone call to the chess club was by the murderer. That means he knew Wallace would be at the club and that the message would be passed on. There was a notice on the wall saying that Wallace was to play a chess match that night – 20 January.
- The killer would have known at what time Wallace would leave the house the next day – the day of the murder, and would easily enter.
- The killer had plenty of time to kill: between 6.45pm and 8.40pm. By witness sightings, Wallace only had twenty minutes to kill his wife and then clean up.
- Money was taken from a cash-box, so perhaps the thief was disturbed and so attacked Julia.
- No bloodstains were on Wallace.
- Wallace's mackintosh was next to the body, and bloody. The killer only had to take it from a hook, and use it to shield himself from blood.
- The missing iron bar by the fire – Wallace knew of it, but the killer would have taken it away.
- Regarding the several blows inflicted, arguably the thief was known to Julia. Hence, he had to ensure she died. It takes two blows to kill, anyway, regardless of who did it or how it was used.
- Wallace checked all other rooms before finding the body – maybe he thought she was in bed.
- There was no money motive – they were comfortably off.

The case for the prosecution

- The call box was near a tram stop. He could have made the call and got to the club quickly. Also, the witnesses said that two tones of voice were used by the caller.
- Wallace could have committed the murder between around 6.30pm and the time he was see on a tram, 7.10pm.
- There was no forcible entry into the house.
- The mackintosh was badly burned in parts. He denied knowledge of owning the coat until closer inspection.
- The multiple blows came from savage intention, a stored-up hatred bursting into a murderous assault

- Searching for the Menlove Gardens address, he rather
  purposefully helped people to remember him if asked later –
  a perfect attempt at establishing an alibi

The crux of the case as heard in court was arguably the visit to
the house of the boy, Alan Close, to deliver milk. Wallace said
he came home from work at around 6.00pm and then Alan
Clsoe came at 6.30pm. Julia answered the door to him. Defence
proved that the boy was there later – actually nearer 6.40pm.
Wallace left at 7.00pm to catch the 7.05pm tram. That is why, if
he had been the killer, Wallace only had around twenty minutes
to kill and to clean up some of the mess.

As to the route and events of the search for Qualtrough's
address, this is the series of actions logged:

1. He asked the tram conductor about the address.
2. Seven other people were asked: these included another
   tram conductor, a clerk walking past him, a person who
   lived at Menlove Gardens West, a policeman, another
   pedestrian, a post office clerk and a newsagent.
3. Most suspicious was perhaps the fact that when he
   talked to the police officer, he made a point of men-
   tioning that the time was 7.45pm.

However suspicious all this might be, the defence had a good
response, as summarised by F J P Veale:

To this argument the defence responded that properly
considered, Wallace's persistence was perfectly natural. He
had had a weary day traipsing dreary streets interviewing
estimable but uninteresting people. He had decided to
devote this evening to obtaining what might prove to be a
valuable piece of business. Having sacrificed his evening
and travelled four miles on a winter's night, he was reluc-
tant to admit that Menlove Gardens East was mythical . . .

It should also be recalled that the tone and vocabulary in the
call itself offered something more unusual than the normal
insurance discussion. The words were: 'I have something in the
nature of his business about which I must talk to him.' That
wording was far from the language used by his usual clients.
Working-class and respectable middle-class Liverpudlians had

been open to all kinds of insurance offers for some considerable time. It was a city in which the First Life insurance firms had sprouted seventy years before. The vast majority of clients for the Pru would have simply rung and said something like, 'I want to talk to Mr Wallace about sorting out some insurance. Could you ask him to call and see me?' Wallace and his colleagues did indeed spend many days walking and riding around the city, paying calls and helping people to understand the workings and the paperwork of insurance. That message – and it was delivered word for word – would have been intriguing. The voice on the phone also used the phrase, 'I want to see Mr Wallace urgently on a matter of business.' That was not by any means a routine call.

One other focus of debate which has to be mentioned is how Wallace behaved when he returned and had difficulty entering his own home. The neighbours, Mr and Mrs Johnston, also came out, and they found him standing in the passage at the back of the house. He would hardly wait there, away from sight, if he was planning to raise the alarm after finding the corpse. Then, when the body was discovered and police arrived, it was noted that, although he sat and smoked, with a cat on his knee (which he stroked), Professor MacFall, who was at the crime scene later, commented that Wallace did not seem at all like a man who had just killed his wife.

The prosecution had a number of pertinent questions to put to Wallace. Perhaps top of the list was why he went on the journey to the supposed client's address without checking. Hemmerde went on the attack:

> Hemmerde: 'You are a businessman . . . you realised that this person who had telephoned the chess club had not the least idea whether you had received his message or not. Yet you go off to Menlove Gardens East?'
> Wallace: 'No.'
> Hemmerde: 'He would have to risk that?'
> Wallace: 'Yes'
> Hemmerde: 'And of course you could have found out at once if you had looked up in a directory where Menlove Gardens East was or was not?'
> Wallace: 'Yes, I could have done.'

But what followed, on closer inspection of his motives for going to find Qualtrough, was that Wallace had had a poor week and he needed to contact the man, saying that the business might turn out to be 'a £100 endowment policy or something of that nature'.

A major factor in the development of the trial was the impressive deportment and control evident in Wallace; but that did not affect the outcome in his favour.

In the early afternoon of the fourth day of the trial, the jury retired to consider their verdict. Their decision was that Wallace was guilty of wilful murder. The judge stated that it was a 'murder unexampled in the annals of crime'.

After the death sentence was passed, Wallace still showed no response. The *Liverpool Post and Echo* reported that 'Wallace's bearing after the verdict was as calm and impassive as throughout the trial, and when asked if he had anything to say, he replied in a quiet tone, "I am not guilty. I don't want to say anything else".'

But that is not the end of the story. At the Court of Appeal on 19 May 1931, his case was reconsidered. This was after his being moved to Pentonville in April, and after prayers being said for him in Liverpool Cathedral. He played the violin, and as death was looming, his violin and his chess set had been brought to him. In Pentonville, though, he was housed in the death cell.

Hemmerde took a long time at appeal to elaborate on how all the evidence stacked against his client was circumstantial. There was a forty-five minute wait for Wallace, before he would know if he were to hang or not. Lord Hewart had found three clear elements which had to be weighed and discussed: first, Mr Oliver had not said that there was no case to answer in the original trial; secondly, was the summing up done with accuracy? Third, as Hewart said, 'The whole of the evidence was closely and critically examined ... The court was not concerned with suspicion, however grave, or with theories, however ingenious.' In using Section 4 of the 1907 Criminal Appeal Act, Hewart quashed the conviction. The summary was:

> It would not have been in the least surprising if the verdict had been the acquittal of the prisoner. It was a case that was

eminently one of difficulty and doubt, but we are not concerned with suspicions, however grave, or with theories, however ingenious. The evidence has not fulfilled the real test of circumstantial evidence – it did not exclude the possibility that someone other than the appellant has committed the crime.

Basically, there must have been an inkling in the mind of the lawyer submitting the appeal application that there was a chink of light, some cause for optimism: after all, in the trial, the judge's summing up had lasted for seven hours. That invariably meant confusion, elaborate explanation, and a certain amount of speculation. The appeal court also had to cope with allegations from Wallace's defence that at the trial the police had been vetting witnesses and jury. Hemmerde, for the Crown, responded to that charge:

> Mr Hemmerde, addressing the court on behalf of the Crown, said that he did not know whence Mr Roland Oliver had got the idea that the jury at the trial were prejudiced against the defence. Mr Oliver had spoken about his (Mr Hemmedre's) speech to a jury in Liverpool. In fact it had been deliberately arranged that there should not be a jury in Liverpool and the jury were drawn from the surrounding country some way from Liverpool.

Mr Justice Wright responded to the charge against the police also, saying, 'So far as the police are concerned, I took charge of this case at least a week before the trial. If this case was pressed, I pressed it. I take full responsibility for everything that was done.'

The last word has to go to Wallace himself. He said, 'I hardly knew what it all meant. It seemed ages before he reached the sentence which conveyed to me the knowledge to step out of the dock, free.'

But the stigma in such affairs does not go away; by the end of 1932, he had moved away from Anfield and he was a sick man, with kidney disease. He died in Clatterbridge Hospital on 26 February 1933 and was buried with his wife in Anfield cemetery. In 1968, a report in *The Times* noted that 'In Anfield, a neighbourhood which has changed little in 40 years, people still talk of him and discuss many strange aspects of the case. He was 'the man from the 'Pru' and as has been pointed out, his employers staged a mock trial before the actual one, and then paid for the defence'.

If the man's innocence is to be confirmed, then it is worth quoting that very skilful and respected crime writer, Jonathan Goodman, who worked on the basis that the milk delivery boy who saw Wallace would not have been there if his bike had not had a puncture. Goodman told the press on the publication of his book, *The Killing of Julia Wallace* (1969) 'While I'm obviously making no charges, I believe the real killer is still at large.'

In the end, all opinions have to cope with the basic fact that Wallace received a phone call from a man who was never traced, and that a street was referred to that did not exist. That one aspect surely leads to the highly likely point that some one wanted the husband out of the house before they attacked and killed the wife. However, as the appeal court session made clear, there were still problems with that: after all, if the man who came to the Wallace home after making the phone call simply wanted to rob the place, what on earth would be his motive for such a murderous and savage attack on Julia Wallace?

Chapter 10

Cornered in Kirkheaton

Anyone who reads the evidence would
conclude that Moore was innocent.

Steve Lawson

T he following few paragraphs tell the established view of a crime in Yorkshire sixty years ago. In 1951, the quiet suburb of Kirkheaton, just a few miles from Huddersfield town centre, was the stage for high drama. At Whinney Close Farm, Alfred Moore had been the focus of a police hunt after a burglary and officers were waiting at his home. Their plan was, of course, to get hold of him with the stolen goods on his person. In the early hours, shooting began from the farm, and two officers went down, mortally wounded.

The man they wanted was inside, and gun-crazy; as the injured men were taken to hospital, the detectives in charge had to make their men remain patient, as they were eager to get to grips with a man who dared to fire on the officers of the law. They were keen to grab him as they knew that DI Fraser had died before reaching the hospital; he had three bullet wounds in him. More police arrived, and it was then a question of how to conduct this siege without more loss of life.

The farm was searched and plenty of goods were found that had almost certainly been stolen; Moore had been approached by Fraser and PC Jagger earlier in the day, and Jagger had seen Moore shoot his officer. An identification parade was held at the bedside of the wounded constable, and Moore was picked out. PC Jagger died the day after this identification. Moore was hanged in Armley on 6 February 1952.

Most reference works have more or less that outline of the events and the killings. As with all historical material, the narrative is broadly accepted and then reproduced, without too much digging into circumstances. Much the same summary of events is given, for instance, in Gaute and Odell's reference work, *The Murderers' Who's Who* (1979) and also in many other general crime reference works.

That all seems very simple and straightforward. But as Oscar Wilde memorably said, 'Truth is rarely pure and never simple.' In fact, the above summary is so far from being an established account of events that as I write this in May 2010, a new investigation into the events of that day is being undertaken. In an article written for The *Huddersfield Examiner* in January, Barry Gibson reported: 'The Criminal Cases Review Commission has announced it will launch a full investigation into the conviction of Alfred Moore.'

The figure behind this move is undoubtedly Steve Lawson, a former detective who has been campaigning for that to be done for many years. Lawson was the man who presented the case to the CCRC. He told the press, 'If the Commission decides that my argument stands, then the case can be sent to the Court of Appeal which can quash the conviction. I would hope that Alfred Moore would then be given a posthumous pardon.'

Before that material given is discussed, it is necessary to review the events of the murder and the trial. On the night of 14 July 1951 a group of ten police officers surrounded the Moore's home, Whinney Close Farm. Alfred Moore was a known burglar, and the reason for the police presence was ostensibly that they wanted their man – he being a well-known criminal in the area. We have to ask why there were ten officers there. The police statements in court made out that shots were fired at the police from the property. PC Jagger, who had been mortally wounded but lived long enough to speak, said that Moore had shot him with an automatic pistol, after seeing Inspector Fraser stagger towards him, also shot, and about to die.

Jaggers's statement was reported in the press: 'Police Constable Jagger stated that he saw Moore at 2.00am on 15 July as Moore was walking towards his farm. He shone his torch in his face, which he saw clearly in the light. He took hold of Moore's arm and Inspector Fraser approached. When Inspector Fraser said, "We are police officers and you are coming with us" Moore replied, "Oh no sir, oh no sir." As soon as he said that, the statement alleged that he whipped out his right hand from his coat pocket and shot him (Jagger) and Fraser.'

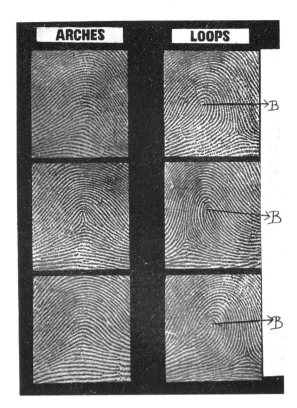

Fingerprints from the early years of their use in forensics. *Police Journal*

Hay-on-Wye from a postcard of c.1900. *Author's collection*

The girl who was the victim in the Donald case. *Vicki Schofield*

The street: Urquhart Road. *Author's collection*

Ethel Major.
Laura Carter

Lincoln Crown Court. *Author's collection*

Norman Birkett. *Author's collection*

Steve Wade who assisted
at the hanging of Rowland.
Laura Carter

HOME OFFICE

Enquiry into the confession
made by David John Ware of the
murder of Olive Balchin in respect
of which murder Walter Graham
Rowland was convicted at Manchester
Assizes on the 16th December, 1946

Home Office
enquiry into the
Blachin case.
HMSO

Report by
MR. JOHN CATTERALL JOLLY, K.C.

*Presented by the Secretary of State for the Home Department
to Parliament by Command of His Majesty
February, 1947*

WPC as Balchin.
Police Journal

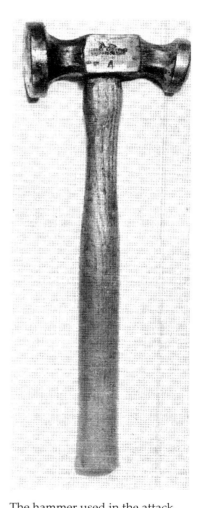

The hammer used in the attack.
Police Journal

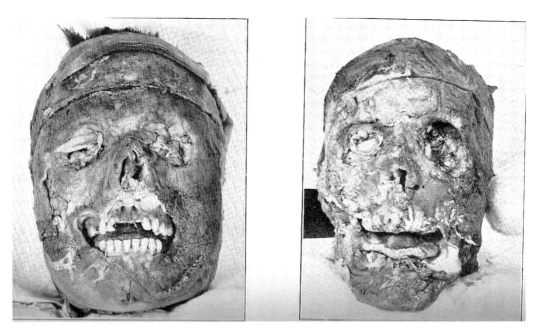

The heads of the two victims in the Ruxton case. *Police Journal*

Wallace.
Laura Carter

The Tynwald, Isle of Man. *Vicki Schofield*

Later, according to police, armed police reinforcements arrived and Moore came out of his farm and was grabbed by the arm. Moore was later charged and his response was: 'How could it be me? I have told you I was not there ... I'm on the spot. I know I am.' After extensive searches, the alleged weapon could not be found, but apparently a number of important items were found in the Moore house.

At the West Riding magistrates' court on 28 August, as Jagger had then died, Moore was charged with a double murder. DCS Metcalfe told the court that in the early hours of 15 July when reinforcements had arrived, he and an armed officer, PC Cleaver, approached the farm. He said that he saw a woman at a window, with a man behind her. He shouted to them and eventually Mrs Moore came out, while Alfred stayed behind, partly behind the door. The officers then walked towards Moore, and he came out and was handcuffed. When told that he was arrested in connection with the murder of an officer he said, 'Oh it is serious ... it's awful!'

Bullets were examined by Dr H A Mays from the Ministry of Supply at Woolwich. He could only say that the bullets in both officers came from the same weapon – more likely a revolver than an automatic. Three cartridge cases were found, and he confirmed that they came from the same weapon.

At Leeds Assizes in December, Moore stood in the witness box and denied any shooting. He said that on the night they were shot he was not concerned with any crime at all. He told the court that, since he had moved into the farm in May that year, he had left his life of crime and had been determined to make a living from poultry farming. He also said that he had never owned a revolver and had no ammunition of the kind described by Mays – 9 millimeter. On the night in question, Moore said that he had been to see his brother, and left him around 11.20pm, and had come back home without meeting anyone. He asserted that he had no gun on his person and did not have a gun when he set out.

The prosecution, led by G R Hinchcliffe, insisted that all the evidence pointed to Moore as the killer of the two officers. He said that the motive was simple – to resist arrest. *The Times* reported that Moore had given himself time to hide stolen goods after shooting the men: 'With the time he gained he was able to destroy a quantity of valuable pieces of jewellery in the cavity wall, to hide the discharged cartridge cases and a live round. It was perfectly true that the weapon that fired the shots had never been found.'

For the defence, H B Hylton-Foster stated that his client was a burglar, not a killer. He told the jury that the prosecution had given no proof that there was stolen property at the farm. It had been raining heavily that night, and yet, he pointed out, Moore's overcoat was 'bone dry' when it had been discovered by police a few hours later. The barrister added that the long and painstaking search for the weapon had been fruitless because Moore did not posses such a thing. There had even been two army teams with metal detectors out looking for the gun, and that had come to nothing.

All that was of no use. On 12 December, Mr Justice Pearson heard the guilty verdict of the jury and sentenced Alfred Moore to death. It had taken the jury just fifty minutes to reach their decision.

Such are the salient features of the case. What strikes us now is just how many unanswered questions exist here. First, why were so many police surrounding the farm that night? Such a massive presence suggests a fear of firm resistance, and in fact also arguably suggests that the officers had a reason to fear being attacked. Otherwise they would have walked up to the door and demanded to see their man, and they would have spoken directly, and made an arrest. It smacks of overkill to say the least. Such a heavy presence hints at a vendetta action. The words 'teach him a lesson' come to mind. At best, it appears like the worst scenes from *Ashes to Ashes* in which earlier and more brutal policing methods were done in the spirit of a gang confrontation.

The problem in defending Moore comes principally from Jagger's insistence that he shone the torch and saw Moore's face, and then that Moore went for a gun. What we don't know is whether or not Jagger knew Moore. How did he know it was Moore? We have no certainty that the constable was acquainted with the man – or even whether or not he had seen photographs. That encounter was reportedly in the early hours, whereas Moore said he had got home by 11.30pm. His only alibi was that of his wife in that respect, and his brother could provide an alibi only up to the return home. It was one man's word against another – and in the case of Jagger, he knew he was dying, so what did he have to lose if he was going along with a fabricated narrative of the night's events, to end his life and career with playing a prominent part in catching a crook?

Then we have the amazing lack of forensics. As the gun was never found, the only forensic statement on ballistics ascertained nothing at all that would incriminate Moore. Why was there nothing done with regard to foot and boot prints? It was a wet night and they were on a track. Shoe or boot prints would surely have given information as to whether Moore did or did not walk out towards Jagger that night?

More fundamental was the accused's character. He had no history of violent crime. Why on earth would he suddenly use a gun so recklessly? He was, or had been up until may, a career criminal. There was no record of armed robbery. He was a 'brain' not a 'brawn' offender.

Now, after these criticisms, it is essential to look at what Steve Lawson has established in his own meticulous research. Lawson has spent years investigating this crime, and what affects the present writer most in this is the horrendous repercussions on Moore's family after the trial and execution. The farm was lost and the family ruined. They had known a good life before the night of the killings: the two daughters in the house were taken to a private school, and the family enjoyed holidays together. That lifestyle could only be maintained in Moore's case by crime – by theft of quite a high order. That explains why there was a determination to catch their man with his booty that night. The only explanation for the police presence that makes sense is that of a determination, as described above, to catch their thief, and to do so red-handed. It was a stake-out.

Lawson is convinced that Moore was indeed in bed at the time. He has spoken to all four of Moore's daughters about that fateful night, and they are convinced that their father was innocent. They have led quiet, anonymous lives over the succeeding years, trying to forget the fact that their father died at the end of a rope. One daughter, Patricia, told Lawson that on that night she woke up to the sound of police whistles, and that she was then bullied into signing a false statement. She spoke to the *Yorkshire Post* and said, 'It has very much affected my entire life ... When I saw him at Armley he asked me to look after mum and she held me to it. He just said he loved us all. Mum was bitter – she didn't really like us to have a life of our own. She had gone from having everything to being absolutely destitute.' After the execution, the family moved away, names being changed.

Tina, a younger sister, spoke to Lawson. She spoke of her mother's struggle to keep the family together. She added: 'I have worried throughout my life that people might find out ... I used to worry about things like that but now I don't. I hope that Steve can get this review and maybe dad can be pardoned.'

The Moore case is a perfect template for that crime story everyone concerned dreads: the hanging of an innocent man. That has been the case with the stories of Timothy Evans and others of course, where circumstances have been complex. But the Moore case is a terrible example of the reach of such a stigma into other lives. Innocent relatives have lives of trauma and shame, when there is no basis for that. In true crime writing, the more everyday repercussions of murder are rarely documented on the side of the supposed perpetrator. The story of Alfred Moore provides that unusual perspective.

Steve Lawson puts his cases succinctly: 'The depositions of all the police witnesses gave an entirely wrong account of what happened and appear to have been manufactured and are mainly untruthful in the contents.' He told the *Yorkshire Post*: 'The Moore family sing from the same hymn sheet in their statements. The police are all over the place. Alfred Moore was a totally innocent man and everybody seems to have forgotten about this case. If there was a public outcry it would be reviewed.'

Hopefully, this critique of the actions taken that night in Kirkheaton will reclaim a story of truth, tragedy and injustice – a major crime story submerged beneath the present-day normality of that Huddersfield suburb. Drivers turn off the road to Lepton after leaving Huddersfield, and arrive at a peaceful bunch of streets with speed-bumps and suburban calm. But even today there is still in Kirkheaton, as in so many small places in the West Yorkshire conurbations, a sense of the rural – of smallholdings, people keeping animals, walks into the country and neighbours walking dogs and talking about local issues. That was the life reformed criminal Moore seems to have wanted. No one who mattered at the time believed him. His past was a weight on him, a burden he could not shift, and his life was destined for a dark, sorrowful closure.

The light of justice is now in the hands of the Criminal Cases Review Commission. Their decision will take time, but Steve Lawson and the Moore family wait with anxiety, stress, and perhaps a tinge of optimism.

CHAPTER 11

A Case of Provocation?
Leonard Holmes

Even if Iago's insinuations against Desdemona's virtue had been true, Othello's crime was murder and nothing else.

Viscount Simon

This is as much a story about lawyers, court rooms and legal technicalities as it is about murder. But the arguments about whether a killing was murder or manslaughter make it a very sensational and important case. It happened over sixty years ago, when thoughts about 'reasonable' behaviour and provocation were more than relevant – they were matters of life or death. If an appeal was lost, the noose waited the person in court.

Leonard Holmes was thirty-one when he came back from the war, and he settled back into family life in 1945, with his wife, Peggy, and their six children in their home in Central Avenue, Walesby, north of Nottingham. On 17 November his parents came to see them and the couple went with them to have a drink at the *Carpenter's Arms*. Everything seemed fine. But that was on the surface. In fact, Holmes had sent a telegram to his lover in Huddersfield, where he had been stationed a few years earlier, saying, 'See you Sunday or Monday for sure. Be prepared. OK All fixed. Len.' May Shaw, the lover in Yorkshire, must have thought that, at last, Holmes was free. She thought Peggy had left him. In a sense she had but that sense of leaving was in death – she had been killed by the man who had smiled and relaxed earlier in the pub.

On Monday 19 November, Holmes and Peggy had a row, based at first on the fact that Holmes claimed some American airmen had been winking at Peggy in the pub. In a rage, he took a coal hammer and struck her. She did not die immediately, but in fact her dentures had slipped into her throat. He took these out, and then, feeling that it was too late for her life to be saved, strangled her. After that, everything he did was as perfunctory as his army duties must have been: he washed, then burned his clothes which had been stained with Peggy's blood, then got the children out of bed to have breakfast and go to school. Somehow, he kept the corpse out of the way, and must have chivvied them along, dismissing questions about their mother. They were told not to come home that night, but to go to grandmother's house.

He then went to Huddersfield to meet May, but set off home again. He never made it to Walesby, but was met by police at Retford. He said to them, 'All right, I know what you want from me.' He was cautioned but spoke again, saying, 'Yes, it happened on Sunday night. It was all over something she said. I hit her with a hammer-head from out of the hot cupboard.'

The statement Holmes gave the next day was to be the basis of a long and complex trial and appeal hearings, all trying to deal with the knotty question of provocation. The story from Holmes was that after the night out, he and Peggy had been in the kitchen when he talked about his jealousy – the winks he thought he saw, and also how he suspected Peggy of having an affair with his brother. In the heat of their quarrel, he said that Peggy said, 'Well, if it will ease your mind, I have been untrue to you, but I have no proof that you haven't at Mrs Shaw's.' Peggy also said that May had been a good friend to them both 'having them at their house'. Holmes' confession was:

> I lost my temper and picked up the hammer-head from the hot box and struck her with the same on the side of the head. She fell to her knees and then rolled lover onto her back, her last words being, 'It's too late now, but look after the children.' She struggled just a few moments and I could see she was too far gone to do anything. I did not like to see her lay there and suffer, so I just put both hands round her neck until she stopped breathing, which was only a few seconds.

Holmes said later that he had seen Peggy's suitcase in the hall, and thought that she was planning to leave him, and that was why he had telegrammed to May. But even leaving that aside as an open question, what came to be the focus of attention in the trial and in two appeal court sessions was what Holmes said at Nottingham Assizes on 28 February 1946: in the witness box he told the same tale, and then this interchange took place:

> Question: 'When you put your hands round that woman's neck and gave pressure through your fingers, you intended to end your wife's life did you not?
> Holmes: 'Yes.'

That simple answer led the judge to direct the jury to ignore the possibility of manslaughter. Holmes had clearly intended to kill, although he made it sound as though it was through mercy, to speed her end, rather than take life in order to complete his murderous attack.

The judge's action at the trial, which ended in a death sentence for murder, became the basis for two long appeal court dramas. First, at three hearings through March and May, and then a session before the House of Lords in July, the learned judges and counsel debated and argued on points of law, sorting out what constituted provocation, and they had to decide whether or not Leonard Holmes had been provoked to act in such a way that the crime of murder might be mitigated.

The theory of provocation with regard to adultery was that a certain action forming manslaughter would be the sight of a partner *in flagrante delicto* – in the act of adulterous behaviour. In Holmes's case, the alleged provocation was simple in the words Peggy had spoken. The heart of the issue was that Holmes had taken two distinct actions: One – he had taken the hammer head and attacked her; and two – he had strangled her to make sure that life was taken.

The line of thought lodged in the appeal judges was that the doctrine of provocation depends on the fact that it causes or may cause, a sudden and temporary lack of control, whereby malice, which is the intention to kill or to cause grievous bodily harm, is negatived (a legal term). As the appeal court report states: 'A sudden confession of adultery without more can never constitute provocation sufficient to reduce murder to manslaughter. In no case can words alone, save in circumstances of a most extreme and exceptional character, so reduce the crime . . .'

This thinking led in the Holmes case to the defence barristers searching the precedents – and there were plenty of these, as 'crimes of passion' are and always have been, plentiful.

Peggy's body was found by Holmes' brother on the day after the killing, when Holmes was in Huddersfield. The telegram had been sent, and Holmes' behaviour in going immediately to his lover looked very black of course. The judge at the assize trial followed the expected course of action in directing the jury to ignore manslaughter, but at the appeal, Holmes' counsel had found a case from 1871 and some later ones which made the appeal worth consideration.

Working for Holmes was Elizabeth K Lane. She and her husband had read law together, and she was called to the Bar in the Inner Temple in 1940. She joined the Midland circuit, and became a QC not long after the Holmes' trial. Her experience with tricky cases such as this gave her good experience: she became a member of the Home Office committee on deposi- tions in 1948, and a county court judge later in life. She and her colleague, P E Sandlands, must have known that a fight to reduce Holmes's crime to manslaughter was a tall order, but they tried. Lane and Sandlands argued that in a possible con- viction for murder, if there was a potential for a defence of provocation, the judge should not direct the jury to discount the provocation argument.

Their argument relied on the fact that Holmes had done two actions: and the essence of their case was: 'Where there is evidence of a provoked attack made by one person on another which consists of more than one blow or other act, it is a question of fact for the jury whether such blows or other acts form part of the same attack or whether, if they do not, the later attacks were due to the same provocation.' They said that it was 'improper' for a judge to direct the jury not to believe what the accused had said, especially here, where there were no witnesses.

In a sense the defence counsel were clutching at straws. Common sense dictates that Holmes, in strangling his wife, had made the decision himself that she was certain to die. He had played God, as it were, in taking a life which may well have been in the balance. On top of that, there was no remorse in him, nor any attempt to put right what he had just done in the hammer attack.

There was a case in 1871 in which a man had been allowed a defence of provocation based on spoken words, but as Viscount Simon at Holmes' appeal said of that case, 'As a general rule of law no provocation of words will reduce the crime of murder to that of manslaughter, but under special circumstances there may be such provocation of words as will have that effect; for instance if a husband hearing from his wife that she had committed adultery, and he having no idea of such a thing before, were thereupon to kill his wife, it might be manslaughter.' But the Rothwell case was different: in that case some tongs were already in the man's hands, and he used them to strike the blow that killed his wife. Holmes had purposely reached for the hammer-head in the box and then used it.

In the end it was stated simply by Simon: the fact was that where the provocation causes an intention to kill 'the doctrine to reduce the offence to manslaughter seldom applies'. The word 'seldom' was what gave Holmes and his barristers a slight inkling of a chance of saving the condemned man's neck. The extensive discussion about provocation was no doubt fascinating to those who attended court and were keen on legal theory. But to imagine Holmes in the dock, his head going back and forth as if he were watching a deadly game of legal tennis, is to contemplate a kind of torture.

The last words uttered in July at the end of the final hearing, which were directly concerned with the case, were that the judge in Nottingham had done the right thing and the appeal was dismissed.

Holmes was hanged at Lincoln prison on 28 May. The hangman was Tom Pierrepoint, and it was to be the last execution he performed. As Steve Fielding has pointed out, Tom was 'walking with a stick and becoming more disabled with arthritis ... the end was moving closer and closer'. The end for Holmes was surely something he must have realised was inevitable from the moment he arrived in Huddersfield, knowing what he had done, and simply fooling his lover that Peggy had left him.

Through all human history, people have killed for love, or so they have reasoned with themselves. Holmes had clearly planned this murder for some time. He had his lover, many miles away, and he had met her in wartime circumstances. The likely thinking came from a romantic and sexual urge: he wanted the new woman and his wife stood in the way. The fact that he had a large family and a good life in Nottinghamshire was pushed to the back of his mind. To call this killing a crime of passion is to lift it beyond the seedy, savage and amoral outrage that it undoubtedly was. If Holmes tried to calculate possible consequences, and even if he played the lawyer and attempted to speculate about creating a scene in which he would be seen to have been provoked, it was never going to stand up in the light of reason.

The court room at Nottingham was definitely a place where reason would prevail, and at the centre of all the subsequent wrangling was the concept of the 'reasonable man' – and the jury surely saw that the man in the dock was in fact a schemer, a monster who would kill his own wife and leave his children to abandonment and emotional distress all for 'love' or what-ever word he might have used. If he had persuaded himself that he was killing for love, then that does not diminish the con-tempt we feel for what he did. Even his expressed and irrational jealousy appears to have come from something weak in him, an element Shakespeare explored in his tragedy of *Othello*, and as Viscount Simon said at the last appeal: 'Even if Iago's insinu-ations against Desdemona's virtue had been true, Othello's crime was murder and nothing else.'

Maybe some would put much of this down to the war – Holmes, along with thousands of other men, escaped the hum-drum life of wife, kids, job and dead routine, for the thrill of a wartime life, when sexual manners and morals were generally more lax. Maybe there was an element on the man that saw the often repeated words, let's do it now, because we might be dead tomorrow, as a licence to push away the thoughts of duty and responsibility that tug at all people in some way. Yet that would be a feeble attempt to explain away a heinous crime. It would ask for understanding, though never sympathy. Holmes deserves no gram of sympathy at all. What began as some form of pathetic weakness grew into a profound desire to kill in order to have what he thought was happiness and freedom.

Leonard Holmes had written the script of a story in his head, considering every twist and turn, and this had simplified people, motives and emotions to such an extent that he could not see the one, massive fatal flaw in the plot: that he purposely took Peggy's life, 'with malice aforethought'.

CHAPTER 12

Guenther Podola

I've a grand memory for forgetting.
R L Stevenson

To understand the twists and turns of this extraordinary murder case, the first step is to reflect on amnesia and what it is. The simple definition, 'loss of memory', will not do. The word is used to cover both partial or total memory loss. It can include the loss of a certain period of time or it can be used to label a condition that is permanent, involving loss of some areas of experience while others are retained. There are several different varieties: in general terms, as an ongoing condition, there is *anterograde amnesia* which is part of the effects of head injuries; the person has problems recalling day-by-day events, though earlier memory may be sound. In contrast there is *retrograde amnesia*, which adversely affects memory previous to a trauma to the head.

Other varieties cover a range of injury and damage. The most elusive, and therefore the most troublesome in a court of law, is *hysterical amnesia*. Here, episodes of memory loss are linked to trauma, and the condition is usually temporary. In other words, it is related to a neurosis, and that may have several causes.

Clearly, a condition of amnesia would cause problems in a murder case, and it certainly did in July 1959 when Guenther Podola was arrested after the murder of a police officer. He was beaten up and there were injuries to his head. The sight of the accused in the dock at the magistrates' court standing before the bench with a black eye was just the beginning of a long and tortuously difficult journey through legal wrangling that awaited the German who had been, almost twenty years before, a keen member of the Hitler Youth and who had become a dangerous gangster.

Some news stories imprint themselves on the consciousness. When I was eleven, our family bought their first television set. It was 1959 and when I wasn't playing cowboys and Indians I was watching adventure tales on television. One of my strongest memories of that summer was hearing the full name – Guenter Fritz Erwin Podola – and seeing a telephone box on the screen during the news bulletin. There was the picture of the man, rough, bruised, as if he has emerged straight from a ruck. He was from the fantasy world of James Cagney and Edward G Robinson. I wasn't the only one who found that the long and strange name stuck in the memory. But ironically, Podola was to claim that nothing stuck in his memory in the period between 16 July and the time of his first trial in September, and it was claimed that he was unfit to plead – something that equated him with an insane person, and therefore, if accepted, that would save him from the gallows.

The Podola story began not long after his move to London from West Germany in May 1959. Previously he had lived in Canada from 1952, and there he had done two jail stretches of over two years for burglary. In London, he took the name Mike Colato, a moniker suggesting a certain mafia or gangland identity, and soon he was breaking the law.

On 13 July that year at some flats in Onslow Square, Kensington, gunshots were heard and residents in that wealthy area came out to see what was happening. They saw the body of a man in the hallway of one flat.

The body was that of DS Raymond Purdy, and he had been there to look into a blackmail allegation. An American model called Verne Schiffmann had had jewellery and furs to the value of £2,000 stolen and she was being blackmailed by the thief – Podola. His call had been traced to a phone box at South Kensington underground station. That was the phone box lodged in my memory. Purdy and DS Sandford had seen the caller, watched him leave the box, and had trailed him to the flats. Podola was aware of them and broke into a run, so they followed. Podola was grabbed and taken to the hall. As Sandford rang the porter's bell in order to get back-up, Podola brought out a gun and shot Purdy.

Residents came to the scene, and one of them rang 999, but it was too late to save Purdy. Podola had run off, so the police hunt was on. At Chelsea police station, the model told the whole story of the theft and blackmail. It didn't take long to track down their man, and a few days later he was cornered at the *Claremont House Hotel*. The detective team with Albert Chambers in the vanguard, battered down the door and Podola was overpowered. He was knocked to the floor, receiving a severe blow to the head. He lost consciousness and he was taken to hospital later – to St Stephen's in Fulham. A statement was issued from there reading: 'Mr Podola was a patient at this hospital for four days. Any information about him is confidential as between him and the hospital. He has a solicitor acting for him and any information will be given to his solicitor ...' But journalists pressed for more and eventually, after Podola was examined by Dr Colin Campbell at Brixton Prison hospital, it was clear that there was a serious problem, because the doctor was a specialist in neurology and neurosurgery. The readers of the popular papers were thinking that he had been brain damaged by the cops after one of their own had been killed.

On 21 July, parliament wanted to know what brutality, if any, had taken place. R A Butler, Home Secretary, said that as Podola was being taken before a magistrate, it would not be proper for him to say anything. But members shouted in protest and one asked, 'What happened to Podola at the police station which necessitated his removal to hospital on a stretcher?' Mr Paget pressed for more, saying, 'I am concerned with the people who beat him unconscious.' Butler replied that Paget had no right to make such allegations and that there was no proof of a beating. Paget shouted that it was intolerable to contemplate 'the idea that one can say *sub judice* to hush up something'. Butler repudiated the whole idea.

But other matters in the news made the general feeling that there had been police brutality more general. One factor in this was that at Purdy's funeral, 1,000 London policemen had lined the last half mile of the route taken by the cortege. The procession was a mile long.

It was also reported that Podola had not been allowed to see a lawyer. Once again, Butler was pushed for an explanation. He said that the prisoner had not asked for one, but that a solicitor had called at the hospital, to find that Podola was unfit to see him.

On 12 August, Podola was due to stand before the magistrates at the West London Police Court. An application for a closed court hearing was given by F H Lawrence, defence counsel, because there had been no possibility of having any information from Podola, who sat in the court, not saying a word. He still had a black eye. The magistrate, E R Guest, made this statement: 'It is now three weeks since this man was arrested and charged. During that time it has been impossible to get any instructions from him about the circumstances of his arrest or the events leading up to his arrest . . . If it still exists at the time of arraignment there will obviously be a preliminary issue . . .' By that he meant that the accused might be unfit to plead.

This issue became on of whether or not Podola, despite the amnesia he was said to have, could still give instructions to his counsel. But following that, a cross-examination would not be possible if the prisoner had no memory of the crucial events of the day of the killing. The defence plea of a 'disadvantage' was accepted. A preliminary hearing, not in open court, was then arranged.

At last the trial began, at the Old Bailey, on 11 September. The fundamental question still was there: the defence put forward a plea of insanity, arguing that Podola had suffered hysterical amnesia for the period in question. The prosecution were sure that the accused was faking it. F H Lawrence, the defence counsel, told the court that his client has completely lost his memory of all events before 17 July that year. It was the first time in English legal history that a defence of amnesia had been argued. Maxwell Turner for the Crown, and Lawton for Podola, took several hours to argue their cases. Much of their discussion was about what constituted 'unfitness to plead.'

Mr Justice Edmund Davies finally said that they could go ahead, and that Lawton would have to satisfactorily demonstrate Podola's insanity. The basis of the argument for the defence was that, stemming from the Criminal Lunacy Act of 1800 (which followed an attempt on the life of George III) there was only one exception to the general rule of 'unsound mind' and loss of the faculty of reason. That was the example of a person charged being a deaf mute. Because that condition would mean that the accused could not participate in the com-munication essential to a trial, it was impossible to proceed.

The question was, could amnesia create the same kind of condition? Would Podola's case be accepted as a condition of insanity? However, *The Times* reported, Lawson's first address suggested an indirect reference to alleged police brutality:

> Mr Lawson spoke of an amount of bloodshed when the arrest was made, and that so far as Podola was concerned it might well be that the scene was one of bloody terror. He observed . . . that much of the blood might only have arisen from slight injuries or even nose bleeding. He added . . . that there was no evidence of any violence having been done to Podola at Chelsea police station . . . But the scene of blood and the shock of his arrest Mr Lawton submitted, might well have been enough to bring about loss of memory . . .

This was clever. Everyone would have been expecting a statement alleging that a beating had caused the amnesia. That would have been too simple. In a sense, he was doing what Shakespeare has Richard III do in the scene in which Richard refuses the proffered crown – deny the obvious by falsely re-strained and underplayed reasoning.

As the trial went forward, the focus was to be on various experts trying to assert or to deny that Podola had amnesia, and if he did, what the repercussions of that would be for the case. This began with the testimony of Dr Shanahan who had seen Podola at the Chelsea station. He said that he 'found difficulty in establishing mental contact with Podola' saying that he had withdrawn as a reaction to his arrest – no more than that. When taken to hospital, Dr Harvey found him to be 'in a stuporous state'. It was beginning to look as though a number of factors were building, the result of which might prove amnesia.

For the defence, Dr Colin Edwards said that Podola's mental condition was normal in all respects, apart from the amnesia, which he confirmed; Lawton challenged the question of a feigned amnesia:

> Lawton: 'There is a problem to decide whether or not a patient is telling the truth?'
> Brown: 'Yes.'

Lawton: 'In what ways are you helped by your medical knowledge in deciding if a man is feigning?'

Brown: 'Firstly we see whether the condition described fits in with recognized disease which one has seen previously . . .'

Lawton asked for more, and Brown described what he would expect to see – emotional stress. Podola at first, when seen by Dr Edwards, said he felt weak all over but had no pain. Then Edwards went into more searching questions about the amnesia. The accused could not recall where he got a scar over his left eye, nor could he recall any jobs he had done earlier in life. Edwards concluded that a physical shock could have been the trigger for the amnesia. Again, Lawton asked Edwards about the possibility of feigning and the doctor said he dismissed the idea of any pretence.

The topic of mental damage – in the sense of harm caused by an attack (by police) had to be faced. Lawton referred to a report by the path lab which said that there was no bruising on the brain, and Edwards accepted that. The judge interposed and asked what a malingerer would do to try to fool doctors and the reply was that 'a malingerer would have been very careful to give an exact reason, chapter and verse'. Edwards told the court that generally memories came back piecemeal and that malingerers 'were very keen to give one symptom which they thought one would expect to find' and the doctor was impressed by the fact that Podola had managed to express one early memory – of being on a railway track the week before. Again, he said that recall came back bit by bit, so that was a convincing sign.

Several experts were called as the days wore on. One of the most interesting was Dr David Stafford-Clark, who had had an extraordinary career in Bomber Command and in popularising psychiatry for the general reader. He had studied stress and mental trauma among servicemen and had been on aircraft raids himself, at one time contracting an asthmatic condition during tests. His testimony set a precedent regarding the admissibility in court of psychiatric evidence, and he was to be called on again the year after the Podola case, to speak at the *Lady Chatterley* trial.

Stafford-Clark could explain aspects of amnesia in terms of describing the effects of trauma. The court (and the general public) really wanted to know if the supposed amnesia had come from a police beating or from the nervous shock of the general violence of the time in which the hotel door was smashed and bodies fell on him. Nothing quite to definite was on offer. But at least the psychologists and general practitioners had made the amnesia seem quite believable.

However, the account of the crime and the events of the day when DS Purdy died tended to counterbalance this discussion with a more emotional and tragic tale. This came from DS Sandford's testimony in court. He said that he and Purdy had acted that day in response to Miss Schiffmann's allegation that she was suffering demands for money with menaces. Maxwell Turner described what had happened in the flats: 'Podola shot Purdy at point blank range through the heart. Under the 1957 Homicide Act, murder by shooting a police officer in the execution of his duty was capital murder.'

On the fateful day, when the two detectives cornered Podola, Sandford told him they were police officers, then he went to the porter, telling Purdy to keep an eye on the prisoner. Maxwell Turner again made it clear to the jury what happened: 'As Sandford spoke to Purdy, Purdy looked towards Sandford, which meant he looked away from Podola. Sandford saw that when Purdy looked away, Podola (who was on a window ledge) put his right hand inside his pocket ... "Watch out, he may have a gun" Sandford said. "He produced a gun from his inside left-hand pocket, fired it at point blank range, and Purdy fell to the ground."'

Podola then ran off down the street. Then, in a search of the *Clarendon Hotel* after Podola was tracked down, police found, in an attic, a purple pullover inside which was a pistol and holster. It was wrapped in a copy of *The Times* for the day Purdy died.

An account was then given of the arrest. DS Albert Chambers, who battered down the door, said, 'I was armed with a revolver and three other officers were also armed.' He said that after he and other officers had taken positions outside Podola's door, they heard a metallic click inside. That prompted him to run at the door and charge inside. Chambers said that he never drew his gun, but that, as was reported in the press, at that time Chambers weighed over 16 stones and 'There was no resistance to him, the door burst open and swung into the room. As it opened he caught a glimpse of Podola ... who staggered across the room and finished up on the floor face upwards, with his head in the fireplace.'

Podola had a cut over one eye and was bleeding. Chambers told him they were police and added, 'Keep still so we can talk to you.' Five officers were then holding Podola down on the floor. He then went limp after a short struggle; he was put on the bed and given first aid, according to Chambers. They sluiced his head with water and then took him to Chelsea police station.

At the end of eleven long and verbose days in court, the jury found Podola guilty of capital murder, in spite of all the medical opinion. The issue about insomnia being a version of an insanity defence had been overridden by other matters. He was sentenced to hang. But there was another long haul through legal language and theory in the appeal court to come. That spanned a week in October in which the case was heard by five judges, headed by the Lord Chief Justice, Parker. The basis of the appeal was this, as expressed by the defence: 'Assuming that the court is satisfied that there was a misdirection on onus of proof on the issue of fitness to plead, it would be open to the appellant [Podola] to say that, on a proper direction, he ought never to have been called to plead and therefore there was a mistrial.'

The focus of debate was the assertion by Podola and counsel that he had no memory of events between 1 July and 16 July and therefore was insane, by reference to the 1800 Act on lunacy. The barristers had searched past cases for precedent and they found helpful trials in cases going back to mid-Victorian times, and even to one in Scotland. Maxwell Turner, for the Crown, put the problem clearly: 'There never has been a case in English law where it has even been contended that amnesia relating to the time of the commission of the offence can render the prisoner otherwise sane and normal unfit to plead.'

The appeal court found that the judge at the Old Bailey had been right to direct the jury to say that Podola had been fit to stand trial. The argument of appeal was based on the fact in the preliminary hearing about fitness to plead, errors were made regarding the allowance for the trial to be undertaken. Lawton had begun the appeal after consulting a classic statement in Matthew Hale's cardinal and influential legal text, *Pleas of the Crown*, which states, 'If a man in his sound memory commits a capital offence, and before arraignment becomes absolutely made, he ought not by law to be arraigned during such his frenzy, but be remitted to prison until that incapacity be removed the reason is that he cannot advisedly plead to the indictment . . .'

In the end, that premise could not be extended to cover the state of amnesia. The appeal was dismissed. The execution was to go ahead, and the date fixed was 5 November that year, 1959. Even then there was still controversy. There were accusations in the press that the hangman, Harry Allen, was a friend of the victim, DS Purdy. The Sheriff of the County of London told the papers that this was not so: 'Mr Allen denies that any such friendship existed and states that he met Sergeant Purdy on just one occasion, which was over five years ago. The Sheriff is accordingly satisfied that Mr Allen is a proper person to act as executioner in this case.'

There was also a petition put together to ask for clemency, as for many the idea of Podola's suffering at the hands of the police made him deserve some sympathy. There was even a mysterious visit from a woman who brought a bunch of violets to the prison where he was to be hanged – Wandsworth – and the flowers were taken in by a warder after a slightly embarrassing pause. The West German authorities also pressed for a reprieve, saying that they did not have a death penalty; that was of no consequence of course, and was dismissed.

Podola was hanged, and the fact that he had killed a police officer meant that the case would be prominent in a number of contexts. In fact, a complete book-length account of the case was in print within a year, by Rupert Furneaux. In 1966, the name of Podola was then in the papers once more, when the Police Federation campaigned to bring back hanging; their argument related to the murder of officers, and their statement included reference to previous cases: there had been three police killings since the abolition of hanging the year before: in West Ham, Carlisle and Wolverhampton. Arthur Evans, of the Federation, said,

As the Federation told parliament when they were discussing the no-hanging bill, a desperate criminal can escape arrest and conviction by shooting a policeman. It is vital to restore capital punishment for the murder of a policeman or to arm them, preferably the former.'

As a coda to the Podola story, it should be noted that Judge Maxwell Turner, who led for the Crown against Podola, died just a year after the case ended. In a classic case of English understatement, the obituary notice said, 'The Podola case was a complex one and many who did not know him were struck by the fairness and clarity of his presentation.'

CHAPTER 13

Late Confessions

The luxury of an intimate confession to a stranger ...

T S Eliot

The following consists of two murder stories from the 1950s and 1970s for which there have been confessions. One has come from a phone call and the other in a letter found with a dead man's possessions. For those reasons, each case opens up frustrating but tantalising questions about events from many decades ago. Such findings are often nothing more than yet further puzzlement in cases which have been problematical from the start. Other confessions may be direct and convincing, but still be open to doubt.

In the first of these stories, the haunting taking of a call by a journalist opens up a long-standing mystery of the savage murder of an aged shopkeeper; in the second, a confession found after death could have given the forensic linguists a tough challenge (and they still did study it of course) but the information there was utterly believable to the cold case detectives. What both stories share is the intriguing potential closure – and so quickly – of matters which have defeated the rigours of investigation and the best police minds of their time and place.

On Whitsun Saturday of 1957, Detective Superintendent Herbert Hannam and Detective Sergeant Rowe, both of the Yard, were on their way north to Halifax. They had been called in by the Chief Constable of the town very soon after the body of Emily Pye was discovered, brutally murdered, in the house behind her grocer's shop on Gibbet Street. Emily, aged eighty, had been severely bludgeoned to death in what one officer described as 'a rain of blows to the head' by a ruthless killer.

The town end of Gibbet Street is today in the heart of the Asian population's community; there is a mosque quite near to the shop which still stands where Emily's body was found all those years ago. The streets around are crowded and busy. The thoroughfare of Gibbet Street leads down to the centre of the town and is always noisy. In 1957, it was not so busy, but it is easy to imagine what it was like then, as the red-brick terraces still stand behind the current establishment, and Back Rhodes Street, in which her home stood and where she was killed, is still there, unchanged.

It was a Saturday when she died. Police later found that the shop and the house had been locked from around 1.45pm. Her body was discovered when her relatives, Mr and Mrs Wilson of Northowram, who had come to invite Emily to spend some of the holiday with them. Doris Wilson was her niece. But they found the premises locked, and through a window Derek Wilson saw the old lady's body, covered with a rug.

The whole investigation was dramatic and high-profile. The forensic specialists came, including Professsor Tryhorn from the Science Laboratory in Harrogate. Crowds gathered to watch as officers stood around talking, or walked through enclosed alleys, before actions were taken. It was a senseless murder, apparently done for a small amount of money taken from the till. It became clear that another, more substantial amount of money was hidden on the premises and had not been found. Superintendent Hannam said he would not have been able to find it. The murder was possibly not done by anyone who knew her, then, and police and police at the time thought that it may have been an opportunity killing by a chance passing casual customer, perhaps en route to Lancashire.

It was unusual for such a high-ranking officer to be there. Hannam was very highly thought of (he will be discussed at length in the next chapter), a smart, dapper man, wearing a Homburg and a very expensive suit. A picture in the *Halifax Courier* shows him almost posing for the camera, looking dignified and impressive. Then forty-seven, he had been a leading figure in many West End cases and had been on assignments abroad.

The affair reached almost mythic status in the area for some time, as the very name 'Emily Pye' as an unsolved murder perhaps done by an unknown assailant resonated through the local community. The woman had been such a popular and warm-hearted person, and had lived alone for fifteen years, but before that had had a 'life-long companion' for thirty years, as long as she had owned the business. At one time when she had been ill and had closed the shop when she was in hospital, she had told her niece that she thought a lot of the customers and ran the shop more as a hobby than anything else. All the more horrible, then, that such a kind and sociable woman should die in that way.

Considerable force was used to kill Emily; it had all the hallmarks of a violent robbery and was representative of a template killing across the country. In the early to mid-1950s there had been a stream of such attacks on lonely women living alone, often on commercial premises. The ultimate irony is that the plain, low-key figure of Emily Pye attracted in her death a media frenzy and a host of law officers who became local celebrities overnight. Such detail was given about Herbert Hannam that readers of the local papers were told that he wore 'designer' clothes and the information was given that his son was highly educated. Hannam was interviewed almost as if he were a figure from a *Boy's Own* hero and much was made of his involvement in monetary fraud in the USA. He was, undoubtedly, a remarkably interesting figure to find walking around a northern industrial town.

But nothing came of the enquiry and it remained unsolved until a death-bed confession given to Calderdale Police in 1988, but the full details of that have not been released. Superintendent John Parker told the *Halifax Courier*: 'This man made a number of anonymous calls. He told the newspaper that his father had admitted to Emily's murder two or three days before he had died. The caller refused to give details because his mother was still alive at the time and unaware of her husband's secret.' The man added that his father had said what he had done was not worth the anguish he had gone through. In 2006, the police again appealed for the caller to come forward with full details, but as yet there is no closure.

Hannam and Rowe had come north, been highly visible, attracted the media, and then returned home.

When a seventy-seven-year-old ex-librarian died in a hospice in 2009, workmen, while looking at the belongings left in the man's room, found an old pistol, a batch of press cuttings and a bundle of yellowing papers on which was written a murder confession. This was in Aspull, Wigan, but it was an apparent solution to an unsolved murder which took place in Liverpool on 2 September 1970, by some binmen, behind the YWCA hostel. On that date, the body of Lorraine Jacob, just nineteen years old, was found. Richardson wrote that late the night before he saw her and approached her, and he recalled that she was carrying three bags of chips; and had just been for a drink at Yates' Wine Lodge. It was 9.00pm and so she was easily spotted by the man with a grudge against her. They had a row, and we know that this was about a camera which the girl had taken from Richardson. They fought, and she was killed.

The confession stated that she had a pawn shop ticket in her purse, and he said that he tore that up. He took her tights and knickers after she died, but there was no sexual attack. At the time, the murder hunt involved 100 officers, but Richardson was never found; he went back to Manchester and continued his life as a librarian. Some 900 witness statements had been taken, and there was even a loudspeaker appeal at a football match at Anfield when Liverpool played Manchester United.

Quite a lot is now known about this academic recluse. Although he lived alone later in life, and simply studied and developed his interests in languages, he had a family – though they were estranged. DS Kemble told the press in 2009 that the confession was written 'in a learned hand with great articulacy … it contained details never made public at the time'. Richardson was a loner; apparently he had some platonic relationships with women and they have said that he was always courteous, and behaved like a gentleman. He had a degree in German and taught himself Russian. He was born in Rochdale, where his father was a chest surgeon.

DNA did link him to the killing, and in a BBC documentary, a former friend of the man said that she had been haunted for the past four decades after she had suspected him but had been too frightened to tell police. The informant said that not long after the killing, Richardson went for a walk with her and told her things that only the killer could have known. She thought that she might be killed also. This partly came from the fact that Richardson read a book about a serial killer and tended to fantasize about doing a random murder. The DNA was only just accessed, because after the finding of the confession, there were only a few hours available before the body was cremated for samples to be taken.

Lorraine's sister spoke for the first time also, in the documentary, saying, 'He took that girl's life . . . she'd two children, a young mother, nineteen. She was only a kid.' At the time, Richardson was working in a restaurant in North John Street and living in Toxteth. He had taken a photo of her child and she and a friend came to his house and took the camera. That seems to have been the root cause of the row that took place. Geoffrey Wansell, biographer of Fred West, has commented that 'It is usually the men who seem the least terrifying who keep the darkest secrets.' This polite and well educated gentleman who lived for his books certainly had a secret: as a neighbour said, 'he was a man who liked to keep to himself' and he also, according to police, expressed no remorse in his written confession. It was not something written to relieve a burden of guilt.

Colin Davies, from the Crown Prosecution Service, told the *Daily Mail* in 2009 that 'Following the forensic evidence and the thorough investigation by the police, I decided there was sufficient evidence to justify a prosecution in the case of Harvey Richardson for the murder of Lorraine Jacob in the event that he was still alive.'

On the day of her death, Lorraine had met a man who, by his own admission, had spent the day getting drunk, after failing some librarianship exams. He wrote that he went to the area to meet some women 'friends' and there he saw Lorraine. Almost certainly, the gentle scholar used prostitutes and also spent time in their company, much as other killers (such as Steve Wright in Ipswich and of course Peter Sutcliffe) did. He may have liked the company of books, and been capable of taking out 'respectable' women for dinner, but his dark side very likely included fantasies of sex and violence. One comment about him in 1970 is that he was 'something of a player among the ladies of Liverpool'.

Did he kill others? Was his fantasy about serial killing fulfilled? There has been some thought that he might be linked to the killings of Barbara Mayo in Derbyshire and Jackie Ansell-Lamb in Cheshire. Is there more to come from the Harvey Richardson story? It seems unlikely, but not impossible, of course. Speculation on him and his lifestyle soon brings up a pattern and a character profile which fit a certain template of serial-killer mentality. So often these psychopaths are Jekyll and Hyde in their social projection of personality, having a dark and dangerous shadow-self; often they develop fantasy and sensual thrill to a point at which there has to be the transgression that the fantasy feeds on.

As to the social front of being a 'gentleman' – well so was Harold Shipman, a supposedly good doctor, friendly and reliable.

People who knew Harvey Richardson will feel a shiver of revulsion as his real story emerges, and there may be much more still to come.

Chapter 14

Devlin and Burns

*Murder most foul, as in the best it is;
but this most foul, strange and
unnatural.*

Shakespeare, *Hamlet*

Cranborne Road hardly evokes a setting for a desperate and confusing mess of a murder, but then Britain is packed with mundane suburban addresses in which the most horrendous murders took place. Most of us probably stroll out to work or to the park every day and walk past a dark place where a life has been forcibly and brutally taken. The ghosts of the victims maybe do not actually haunt these places, but once the back story is known, we take a second glance at them and wonder about what went on inside those remarkably bland-looking walls. Cranborne Road evokes afternoon tea, a spot of gardening, and nothing more exciting that a chat about the latest score from Lord's. But anyone in Liverpool with a sense of its more eventful history will feel a quiver of unease at the name.

Syd Dernley, the hangman, wrote in his book, *The Hangman's Tale*, a neat paragraph that with hindsight is a wonderful understatement about this case:

> . . . The double execution was at Walton prison in Liverpool and went ahead amid extraordinary fuss and uproar from people who protested right to the end, and indeed, beyond, that we were hanging two innocent boys.

The furore he refers to had involved a high-profile enquiry into the possibilities of a miscarriage of justice. The two 'boys' in question were Edward Devlin and Francis Burns; they had been accused of the brutal murder of Mrs Beatrice Rimmer in her own home at Cranborne Road, Wavertree. There had been word in the neighbourhood that Mrs Rimmer had been left a lot of cash by her husband and, as was a common habit in those days, she had not banked it, but kept it somewhere at home.

On 19 August 1951, she came home late and as she opened the door and stepped inside she saw that two men had tailed her and now stood before her, ready to do some harm. They set about their victim with a piece of wood and she was brutally beaten to death. Mrs Rimmer took a long time to die, but amazingly no one in the neighbouring houses heard any disturbance. The next night her son came to see her, and he had the terrible experience of peeping through the letterbox to see the body of his mother outstretched in the hall. She was lying in her blood, still clutching some flowers she had bought the day before. The poor victim had a dozen head-wounds. The overall number of wounds on her body was fifteen, and that two weapons had been used. The killers had not been able to find the supposed money and it had driven them to a wild fury. They had broken in through a window.

There was a network of communications on the streets in a crime of this nature, and information soon led officers to the two young men, Manchester criminals: Devlin, twenty-two and Burns, twenty-one. They claimed that they could not have done the killing because they were doing a 'job' in Manchester that night. But there was a host of people with witness statements about the men, and they were charged.

The celebrated Liverpool detective, Herbert Balmer, went to talk to Burns's girlfriend, Marie Milne (known as Chinese Marie) and she told a tale of her being involved as a look-out but then that plan was abandoned later. It was also discovered that one early plan had been to use a local woman called Bury, who figured later in the enquiry, to go to Rimmer's front door and keep her talking while the two men went in through the back and looked for the cash. Obviously, for the fortnight between them being heard to talk about the robbery on the train and the day of the murder, a number of ideas had been discussed.

At their trial, they relied on naming a range of other characters who were allegedly trying to spread the blame; they were arrogant and abusive, both to the judge and jury. The public gallery was packed with curious citizens and there were long queues outside on the last day of the ten days of the trial, eager for the verdict. For defence the men had Rose Heilbron and Noel Goldie – a formidable team.

The defence case rested mainly on the alibi that the two men were in Manchester at the time of the murder. They had three testimonies to back that up: a statement made by Elizabeth Rooke, a confession made by Joseph Howarth and other information, gleaned from other people (one in Walton gaol at the time).

But the sheer conceit and bad behaviour of the accused was going to be an obstacle to effective legal work in the arena. But their expertise was to be tested later; at first the verdict was guilty and Justice Finnemore put on the black cap.

The case went to appeal and failed, but then, on 27 February 1952, the Home Secretary, Sir David Maxwell Fyfe, appointed Albert Gerrard QC to lead an enquiry to see if there had been a miscarriage of justice. This sprang from Rose Heilbron's handing a copy of a statement to the appeal court judge, and he said, 'It may be a matter for the Home Secretary in certain events.' The reason for this was that there were dozens of people involved who had all given garbled or partial statements regarding both the alibi of the Manchester robbery and about the possibility that the men had been framed. *The Times* reported the announcement in dramatic terms:

> The Home Secretary has appointed Mr Albert Dennis Gerrard to inquire into the statement made on 27 March 1952 by Elizabeth Rooke to the effect that June Bury and other persons had told her that the prisoners . . . had not committed the murder . . . and that it had in fact been committed by another unnamed person who is alleged to be the father of Bury's child . . .

The aim of the enquiry was primarily to look into this statement made by one Elizabeth Rooke, the confession made by Joseph Howarth that he had done the murder and a batch of other statements made to officers and to prison staff. Gerrard stated that she was lying. As *The Times* reported about this woman's testimony: 'She knew or believed that the father of that child was one Edward Duffy, and that he was in prison at the time of the murder.'

The problem for the inquiry was just how substantial the narrative put together by June Bury was. She said that she had first met Burns at a pub called 'The Dive' in Liverpool and that she had heard Devlin and Burns, as they sat in a café, plan a job. They said that this job was at a house where an old woman lived alone. Bury also claimed that on a train journey from Liverpool to Manchester, she had heard the two men have a similar discussion about the same job. The prosecution at the trial made a strong argument that both conversations were about the Rimmer break in and murder.

Gerrard, in his special inquiry, had to chase up the stories. He said in his report that he went out and did some detective work of his own:

> I thought it desirable to try to establish if Rooke, Joan Porter, the unidentified girl whose name might be Margaret, and June Bury had been resident in the Upper Duke Street Girls' Hostel, Liverpool, at the same time, and if so, when. I was assisted in this investigation by Mrs Wilkins, an organiser at the Girls' Welfare Association, an official at that hostel.

He was right, records showed that all three girls, Rooke, Porter and Bury had been at the hostel at the same time in October 1951. The Bury story was seen with suspicion as a fabrication. But further investigations took place, and statements were verified, mainly the fact that the man with a name like 'Aussie' whom she referred to was actually traced. If she could be believed on these matters, then her story was worth listening to.

At the Court of Appeal it emerged that a teenager, Rooke, had made allegations about the probity and reliability of the key witness, June Bury. The basic facts about the case in terms of prosecution were that the men had planned the robbery on a train journey from Manchester to Liverpool, as Bury had said, two weeks before the attack and murder. Another woman witness had stated that she had been with the men for three days around the time of the murder and had left them at the time of the break-in. Despite these accounts, the defence counsel were still seeking to establish that the men had the Manchester alibi: that they were breaking into Sun Blinds of Great Jackson Street on the night of the murder. There were six major statements to be checked out, most notably a supposed confession.

This had been made by Howarth. He had said that he had been in the home of Mrs Rimmer that night and had been hidden in a cupboard, waiting for her return. He said that he jumped out and hit her when she came home. It didn't take Gerrard long to dismiss this. Not only local police but Jack Spooner of the Yard had been to check this, and Spooner had made it clear that the only cupboard in the place was under the stairs, and on the murder night it had been full of household appliances – objects that had not been moved for some time, and so were in that space on the fateful night.

Howarth was in the opinion of Gerrard, giving the court the 'stuff of pure invention.' All through the enquiry, Gerrard made comments about how he formulated judgements about the reliability of the various statements.

Another player in the drama was one McLoughlin. Devlin had written a petition in which he claimed that when he had been picked out and his arrest confirmed, McLoughlin had been given a physical description of them both by a confederate called Milne. Devlin said that he had never seen McLoughlin, ever. But McLoughlin had been in Walton for several days, and had made judgements at two identity parades. How did he get the prior information about the two men if he was inside?

In Walton prison, more important information was gathered by Gerrard, about the alibi of the two men being in Manchester. Gerrard went to speak to the governor, and there was valuable information given by a prisoner, 'X', about the construction of the alibi. Mr 'X' said:

> ... Devlin told him that the trial was going all right for him ... Devlin further told 'X' that whilst in prison he had learned every little detail from the man who had committed the Manchester warehouse breaking ... of how that crime had been carried out, and that he had procured this man to support his, Devlin's, statement that Devlin had taken part in that crime. 'X' stated that Devlin boasted to him how they had built up the alibi ...

Was 'X' telling the truth? Gerrard had no doubt when he interviewed the prison Governor, Sheed, because Sheed had visited Devlin in the death cell. He said that Devlin had said, 'If I win my appeal at the Appeal Court on Monday will I be arrested by the police?' When asked why he said that in the trial he had admitted doing the Manchester job. But Devlin added that that was all false, saying, 'Of course we did not do the job.' Devlin later tried to recant that, even to quibbling about the punctuation in the way that the Governor had written it down. This alibi was the difference between life and death, so Gerrard had to check out all details with all available parties. He spoke to Allan Campbell, who was supposed top have done the Manchester break in with the two men. He confirmed that yes, they had done that job together.

Gerrard was nothing if not thorough. He checked Campbell's account of a part of that break in where they sorted out using a lorry or a wagon to take away the stolen goods. The replies to questions in the trial differed considerably from the answers given to Gerrard.

Later, it emerged that Howarth had recanted his 'confession' as well; he was asked why he had told a pack of lies and could only reply: 'I heard a lot of people saying he was innocent and I sort of believed that he was innocent myself.' To DS Newton, Howarth said, 'I was canned up when I said it. I've never seen Burns in my life . . .'

Under all this complex investigation, one important fact counted most profoundly: Gerrard concluded that June Bury had not been telling the truth when she said she had never made statements about the two men while she was in the Liverpool hostel. She was also lying when she said the murder was done by the father of her child ('Aussie'). Really, she knew that the father of her child was called Duffy, a man in prison at the time of the murder. As for Howarth, Gerrard reported that his reasons for the confession were 'confused' and that everything he had said was pure invention.

The die was cast. Nothing in the long enquiry changed any opinion of the appeal judgement. The two men were to hang, and they had their appointment with Syd Dernley. It must have been a momentous statement when Mr Gerrard gave his decision:

I have examined this relationship very carefully. As a result
I have to report that in my opinion there has been no miscarriage of justice.

The very last gambit from the killers' lawyers was a memo-
randum begging for a reprieve from Her Majesty; this came to
nothing. They were not quick in doing that. After all, it was
quite a challenge after the inquiry, to decide on what grounds a
reprieve should be asked for. Locally, there were still voices
clamouring for a revision and that the men were innocent; then
there were rumours in the popular press that the men had made
death-cell confessions.

Dernley recalled that in their cells, the men were 'trying to
play the hard men'. It's hard to believe, but he reported that
even in the death cell, Burns was planning revenge on those
who had spoken against him. On 25 April they were hanged.
Apparently Devlin started to weaken near the end and the
tough image dissolved. As for Burns, he was, said Dernley,
putting up a front until very near the end.

Even this was not the end of this saga. On 19 May, one
G Rowland wrote to *The Times* after reading about the Lords
discussing the point that the Court of Criminal Appeal should
have the power to order a retrial. He wrote: 'The surprising
thing is that the Lord Chancellor said that any legislation to this
end would certainly be controversial.' Then he added, '. . . who,
I would ask, is against this salutary reform?'

The two young killers had not only stirred up public indig-
nation and created more open discussion of the death penalty,
they had also pinpointed the odd process of having to ask the
Home Secretary to order an enquiry into a possible miscarriage
of justice. The result of that inquiry was the cause of a major
statement by Lord Goddard, Lord Chancellor, in the House
of Lords. He was not happy with the separate judicial inquiry
headed by Gerrard. Goddard referred to the Criminal Appeal
Act of 1909 saying that there should have been a retrial of
Devlin and Burns, or at least a prosecution of Bury for committing perjury. The source of the debate was a letter from the
Director of Public Prosecutions to the inquiry administration:

I consider it right, in the circumstances, that the Secretary
of State should know, for the information of the tribunal,

that no prosecution will be instituted by me based upon evidence given to the tribunal in respect upon any matter relevant to the terms of reference. Moreover, I will not make use, and will take such action as is open to me to ensure that no use is made as evidence in criminal proceedings, of any relevant information which may be given to the tribunal.

Goddard pointed out that that letter gave Gerrard *carte blanche* to gather any information at all on the case, and be able to promise that whatever was said to him, no proceedings would follow. That is why everyone spoke to him so freely. Goddard expressed the problem very clearly: 'If June Bury had committed perjury, if the findings of the commissioner had been different, should she not have been prosecuted for swearing a man's life away?'

The separate inquiry by Goddard became a White Paper, no more. In other words, it was something totally outside the courts system, and Goddard was right to make a furore about it. The purpose of the appeal was to decide whether there had been a miscarriage of justice. It had no power to order a second trial, but could only allow or dismiss an appeal. In other words, in the end, the Gerrard inquiry was really irrelevant to the situation of the condemned men, and was more about perjury and false confession. It was, in effect, tying up loose ends. As the debate was continuing on the inquiry, Devlin and Burns were waiting to die.

Behind all the debate and the letters to the papers, though, what remains as the powerful image of the Cranborne Road murder is the gallery of faces showing the people involved: Burns' photograph shows a hard face with set, firm lips; Devlin has a face reminiscent of the Teddy boys of the era. Finally, in the records there is the sad, ironically happy face of Mrs Rimmer, wearing a formal hat and smiling broadly.

CHAPTER 15

Homer and Standen

All cases of remarkable courage, bravery
or intelligence shown by constables in the
discharge of their duties will be reported by
the Superintendents in charge of Divisions
. . . such reports are kept at the Chief
Constable's office.

Constabulary Handbook, 1915

In 2000, PC Joe Holness of Kent Police researched the subject of the killings of police officers on duty. He discovered to his amazement that there was no special commemoration in practice. As he told the *Police Review*: 'I found it astonishing that there have been so many officers who have lost their lives on duty and yet there is no fitting National Memorial Day for them.' He went to work to put matters right, and in 2004 the first such event was held. What spurred him into this research was the death of his colleague, PC Jon Odell in 2000.

From the very beginning of the Metropolitan Police and the first professional force in 1829, officers died on duty, and by violence. Apart from murders of officers in the Bow Street Runners, the first police killing after the 1829 Act was of PC Joseph Grantham who was on patrol in Somers Town. He went to intervene in a quarrel involving two drunken Irish men arguing over a woman. When Grantham went to them, he was knocked to the ground, kicked on the head and body and left to die.

That was the first, but the murder of officers goes on. It is not hard to find such cases from the past, but it is worth asking under what circumstances do police murders tend to happen? Most often, they happen because the criminals are desperate, cornered and exceptionally keen not to go to prison. Debates could continue all day about what would constitute a deterrent, but the question arises about what makes such killings 'famous but forgotten'. Sadly, the deaths of police officers are soon forgotten by the media; the public will read the report in the paper, feel sad and express sympathy, but then life will go on and another murder will soon follow.

The following case from 1982 illustrates one aspect of these categories of killings, and it does not make educative reading: it is as senseless as could be imagined.

It might seem highly incongruous to mention Hollywood in connection with the company of Chamberlain Phipps Wallpapers Ltd, of Bishop Auckland, but in March 1982 a gunfight outside their factory was like something from a gangster film. There had even been a shout of 'This is a stick-up!' When the police arrived not long afterwards less than eight shots had been fired and the two robbers got away with £5,000 in wages money. In fact, the two men who figured in the following story would seem to illustrate Shakespeare's words about his tragic hero, King Lear: 'He hath ever but slenderly known himself.' The main difference here being that the two men who ended up behind bars were far from being tragic heroes: they were everyday, despicable criminals with no regard for human life.

The problem was – and this is where the glamour fades away into the grey reality of County Durham – Constable James Porter of the Durham Constabulary was killed that day. It was one more tale of a gunfight in a country increasingly troubled by this type of criminal activity. Only the day before, police had shot a man in a Essex robbery and, in the popular dailies, this was reported alongside the episode of violence in Durham.

Unusually for such a crime, the motive behind this loud and reckless day of murder and robbery was a grudge held by the two men involved, together with a highly charged political atmosphere in an era when strikes were commonplace and there was frequent unrest in the workplace. Two men, Eddie Horner and Paul Standen, were in their twenties; they were very close, and part of their friendship was a sense of allegiance against the capitalists they believed were exploiting workers. It has to be remembered that at this time reading Karl Marx was *de rigeur* in student communities and in young people everywhere who saw the inequalities all around them. The friends had been involved, as so often at that time, in unofficial strike action and had been sacked as a consequence of this.

But these two were not just going to simmer away, bearing their grudge and reading socialist books – they had an urge to create mayhem and take some direct action. That meant breaking the law and taking some risks. The plan was that they would be driven to the factory by Thomas Bright, a fifty-two-year-old who had also lost his job with the firm. They would then pull on balaclavas, take the money in time-honoured fashion by creating fear and a great deal of noise, and then escape. It worked as they had planned, but Standen was enjoying pulling the trigger. As they left with a sack of money, a foolhardy salesman refused to lie down and had the presence of mind to take in some details of the attack. As they made their getaway, running across a field, Standen fired at the works manager.

The plan was going badly wrong. If they had expected it to be easy, they were very wrong. The alarm system and some phone calls meant that two police officers, DC Porter and DC Simpson, were quickly dispatched into the surrounding area to look for them. They were in plain clothes and they left their unmarked car to approach two men walking towards them. Their mode of address was casual, as Porter asked if they had seen 'two lads further down the lane'.

They were the last words DC Porter spoke. Homer shot him from close range, the bullet from the Magnum going right through his chest. Homer then shot at Simpson but missed. In a desperate ploy to avoid the same fate as his colleague, Simpson pretended to be injured – and it worked. The two men took Porter's car keys and fled, knowing that there would be more police arriving soon. But the film scenario was not over yet. As in many a scene from *The Sweeney* on television at the time, another police vehicle, driven bravely by DC Brian Stewart, smashed head – on into the villains and Stewart was fortunate to receive only minor abrasions. He ran out to face the gunmen and found that he had the element of surprise on his side. Homer was unconscious and Standen, although ready to use the gun, was pointing it away from Stewart at that moment. The officer grabbed for the gun while using Homer as a shield. Stewart then stood on Standen's hand and waited for assistance. Standen later said that Stewart was 'a brave bastard' and he summed up his attitude to the world and to the desperate crimes he had committed when he added, 'Up the revolution!'

The driver, Bright, was arrested later on. At the trial, Standen said, naively, that he had never expected anyone to be hurt in the attack. To back up this shallow and somewhat childish attitude, he referred to taking up a 'two-handed combat stance' to deter the manager, who was thinking about approaching them as they made their getaway. He claimed that he had really wanted to give himself up when he saw the car with the detectives stop in the lane. It does seem true that it was Homer who was the one who 'lost it' – Standen said that he thought his friend 'flipped, gone berserk'.

The fact is that Standen had put his gun away before the fatal confrontation with the officers. His story was believed by the jury. Homer and Standen got what they wanted from each other – partnership and fantasy. What made one the heartless killer and the other a more fearful partner will never really be explained.

It was a particularly tragic affair as DC Porter had a young family. Despite being shot so close and with such a powerful gun, he did not die immediately but in the ambulance on the way to the hospital. He had lived in Meadowfield, County Durham, and he was just thirty-one.

Standen's attitude at the trial at Teesside Crown Court was firm, unemotional and without a dash of remorse. He told the court that he did not recognise its authority and that he was 'guilty and proud of it'. Both men hated their own society and Eddie Homer spoke as if he were living in a weird inner world of fantasy, saying at one point, that he wanted to be 'like Carlos the Jackal'. Standen was described in court as a drifter who was on the fringe of the Socialist Party. He was sacked after being on a picket line during a one-day strike. He had even been in a group of activists who visited the House of Commons a few weeks before the murder and, while there, he shook hands with Michael Foot.

Standen's story is typical of so many disenchanted individuals. He was raised in a council house in Polegate, East Sussex, where he lived a repressed childhood with an authoritarian father. When he grew up, he joined the army, enlisting with the Royal Signals at the age of twenty-one. But this lasted only a few weeks and he became one of the mass of casual labourers who moved across the land, doing temporary jobs. In 1980, he was in Durham, and there he met Homer, who was a kindred spirit who enjoyed radical talk, imaginative speculation about 'revolution' and Socialist theory. Homer was, at that time, a steady worker, but together they formed a dangerous politicised unit and became obsessed by leftist militancy.

In December 1980, talk turned to the perilous business of buying a gun. It cost them £138 and possession of it justified their description as 'two violent and ruthless men', as David Savill QC expressed it at Teesside Crown Court. They became 'joined at the hip' in their bizarre plottings and dissent against any state or other related authority. When the one-day strike came along in September 1981, Bright and Homer were sacked, along with many more men and this rankled deeply. Oddly, it was when the two men went south to spend time in Eastbourne that they hatched their plan of armed robbery.

Homer was from Woodhouses, St Helen Auckland, and the driver, Bright, hailed from Oakley Green. Bright was given a five-year sentence for aiding and abetting but was cleared of manslaughter. As discussion progressed and the details were revealed, it became clear in court that the two gunmen were to be severely dealt with. Eddie Homer was convicted of murder and ordered to be detained for life with a recommendation that he serve twenty years. Standen was found guilty of manslaughter and given two concurrent twelve-year sentences.

It would be possible to take a broader view of cases such as these, gun crimes by people who should never have been allowed near any weapons at all, even toys, and say that the perpetrators were victims of fantasy, that their Socialist dreams mixed with the wild west fantasy land of B movies and their stagecoach hold-ups. But in truth, a reality check should have come to them well before a gun was pointed at a police officer and fired.

The memorials go on then, memories of officers who died doing acts of bravery. In this case, as in so many, facing the barrel of a loaded gun was just another sentence in the job description. Fantasy is one thing, but in the end, this is a story of a heist that was planned: to implement such a design, actually intending to rob and to carry a lethal weapon, was a matter of hard fact, and with hard consequences.

CHAPTER 16

Appeals and Doubts

The punishment of a criminal is an example to the rabble; but every decent man is concerned if an innocent person is condemned.

Jean de la Bruyere

search through the archives in search of a criminal record can be a frustrating business; sometimes the material is spare and there is very little to explore. But other searches may yield a real embarrassment of riches and in the case of appeals from the condemned, the sense of importance, and of the desperate work done by the lawyers involved, is great. Such is the last phase in the story of Mary Daly.

Some cases of homicide are particularly complicated with the problem of finding out exactly what the circumstances are that led to a violent death. If we have a death in which two people struggled and grappled in extreme passion, with no-one else present, then everything in court is going to rest on exactly what went on and who did what. Today, with the modern sophisticated techniques of forensics applied to materials at the scene of crime, a detailed narrative of events leading to a death may be constructed with scientific support. But sixty years ago, when two women fought in a Dublin church, there was uncertainty as to exactly how the struggle resulted in a death.

The fight happened in the Glasnevin church of Our Lady of the Seven Dolours. The church has now been replaced by a more modern building so again, we have to imagine the scene and its physical environment, but what happened was that Mary Gibbons, who was eighty-three years old and lived in Botanic Avenue, walked to church in August 1948, as she did every day. She walked through a warm summer day to the dark interior of the church and there she found a pew and began to pray. She was near the confessional, but was completely alone in the church, at least until the door opened again and someone else came in. The door closed after a beam of light had shot in momentarily.

Then we have another woman's story before we find out what happened in the church. Mary Daly was very hard up. Her landlady said that she was living at this time in lodgings with her husband and child, in Botanic Road. They had a struggle to find the weekly rent. Mary had been to beg money from a priest, things were so bad, and he had given her the cash for the week's rent. But it was always going to be a constant battle to survive. In desperation, Mary went to the church in Glasnevin that day, but she had a hammer in her shopping bag. Her motives will always be a mystery, but the fact is that she went to the church with that potential murder weapon.

As Mary Gibbons prayed she was suddenly aware of a crack on her head. She was a large woman, well-built and still with some strength in spite of her age. After an initial sense of sheer stunned shock she turned to find Mary Daly, who was small and lightly made, wielding a hammer in the light of the church candle. One second she had been saying her *hail Marys* and the next she was fighting for her life.

Mary grabbed Mary Daly's hand and the fight began. Mary Gibbons was bleeding profusely and she broke away and ran to the door of the church to cry for help but more hammer blows were slammed on her head. There was a trail of blood from the pew where the attack began, right to the door.

Some children came to church at that moment and they heard the cries and screams inside, so they decided to run for help. A local butcher called James Canavan and a lorry driver, Thomas Mitchell, rushed to the scene and they had to force open the door, as one woman was lodged against it. When they got inside, Mitchell immediately realised he had to snatch the hammer from the smaller woman, and he did so, while Canavan tried to help the old lady in her pain. What happened then could have been the scene of any small-scale street brawl in Dublin, something not that uncommon. But it was the beginning of the confusion set before the forces of law in court, because a crowd had gathered, including the children, and what they saw and heard was not a hammer attack from behind but two women screaming, accusing each other of violence.

Old Mary Gibbons naturally told everyone that the younger woman had attacked her, but Daly then retorted with an accusation that Gibbons had tried to rob her and snatch her handbag. Detective Sergeant Joe Turner then arrived and that was the scene of noise and confusion he saw, in a most unseemly place. An ambulance was called and Turner questioned Daly, who insisted that the old woman had tried to steal her bag. 'I was struggling with her to get my bag back!' she said.

As for Mary Gibbons, who was in hospital as Mary Daly was carried off to the police station, she was very seriously injured. Her skull had several wounds and bones were cracked; but she was able to give evidence in a special court held in the hospital of Mater Misericordiae in Eccles Street. It was to be a period of uncertainty for all concerned, mainly because the victim was confused about the actual events in the church. There was no confidence in her medical condition being either one thing or the other. At first, the doctors thought that she was pulling through and so when Daly stood before Judge O'Flynn on 16 August, the charge was wounding with intent, not attempted murder. But that was to change. At first the old lady was thought to be 'out of danger' but within a day she was dead. Back came Mary Daly to court to face a murder charge.

The trial was on 8 November at the Dublin Central Court. From the accused's home and family situation there came a motive, put together by the counsel for the prosecution, Sir John Esmonde. The financial difficulties of the Daly family (with a young baby to support) meant that facts were uncovered that showed how desperate Mary Daly would be to get hold of some money; there had been a court order served on her to pay her rent. It was in the Church of the Seven Dolours that a priest had given her money just a short time before the attack, so it was an easy matter to find a motive in her return to that church in such dire straits. Was she carrying the hammer in case she had to extort money with threats this time, as opposed to begging and hoping for further largesse from the priest? That seemed to be the case.

The issue was, as there were no witnesses, whether or not Mary Daly went to the church with an intent to kill for money or whether there were other reasons for what she had in her bag that day. Testimony from the lorry driver who saw her that day and who restrained her, Mr Mitchell, was that Daly was distressed and excited, and that she did say that the hammer, which she had bought in Woolworth's store, was hers; similarly, the children in court, who heard the attack but did not see it, said that they did hear a voice saying, 'Help . . . she's murdering me!' So who was doing the attacking?

Mary Daly was small and the older Mary Gibbons was tall and well-made; that was a factor that complicated things of course. Daly's defence argument was still that Gibbons had taken the hammer and attacked her; she may have been just 5 feet 2 inches tall and delicately made, but in the end, who had the clear motive? Why would the old lady have attacked Daly? The defence brought in a medical expert to say that the accused was so frail that she could not have used a hammer, and on the matter of her financial straits, Daly said that she did have £5 on her that day, and that the old lady was intending to steal that from her. The lengthy defence narrative was the familiar one of self-defence, creating a story in which Daly, going into the church for quiet prayer and carrying her bag and purse, was attacked in the semi-darkness and that she happened to have the hammer with her and so she used it. That does not sit easily with the statement that she was too delicate to use a hammer.

The contradiction and confusion continued as Daly claimed that she had only at first hit Gibbons on the arm, that the old lady took the hammer and turned on her; being the stronger, she argued, the old lady then set about whacking her about the body with the weapon. She said, 'I tried to get out the door. I could not as the woman was leaning against it. I kept shouting for my husband for help. I thought I heard footsteps outside. I gave the woman another blow of the hammer on the head . . . I did not know where I was hitting her. I hit her to get rid of her.'

The defence really dramatised this situation with great emotional emphasis, saying, 'Anyone who found themselves in Mrs Daly's position would probably have acted as she had done. There was no criminal intent.' But the judge pointed out that Mrs Gibbons had been praying and so that small as she was, Daly would have approached the old lady from a position above. That was a hypothetical detail that had some influence on the jury, who were out to deliberate for an hour or so and came back in with a guilty verdict, though they recommended mercy. But the sentence was one of hanging, with a date fixed in December that year.

The final chapter of this case is one of an incredible series of appeals; a date for appeal was set and then everything depended on points of law, mainly that the deceased had made a formal 'dying declaration' regarding the attack (at that time only one of minor assault of course) and that such a matter could not be admissible in a murder trial. In an example of what must have been a desperately stressful situation, the judges rejected this but then opened up the possibility of a final appeal to the Supreme Court. There was then a complete re-trial because of legal technicalities, and again the judgement was guilty of murder. For a second time Mary Daly stood in court and heard her death sentence. But the string of frustrating and dramatic trials ended there, as shortly after that second decision her sentence was commuted to life imprisonment. Mary did a seven-year stretch, followed by time with a religious order, and then went back into her life.

The start of her prison stretch coincided with the first implementations of Sir Samuel Hoare's new Criminal Justice Act, which was created in July 1948. That meant that as Mary went into her cell, reforms were about to be put in place: corporal punishment was to be reduced, penal servitude was abolished, imprisonment with hard labour ended, and there was a new classification of prisoners into three divisions. Small concessions to the tough regime had been made throughout the 1940s, such as smoking being allowed by long-term prisoners in 1947, and visits and letter writing were given more freedom to operate.

But the attitudes to the death penalty remained. Yet still there was clemency. A typical attitude to capital punishment was given by Sir Thomas Molony in a paper he read in 1948: '... in 1922 it fell to my lot to deal with the accumulation of crime from all parts of the country at the Commission Court in Green Street. The country had been in a very lawless state ... I had eighteen cases of murder to try ... in seven distinct cases verdicts of murder were returned and I sentenced each of the prisoners to death, as I was bound to do ... In four cases the prisoners were hanged . . .' In that same year, another Irishman, George Bernard Shaw, had written a critical piece on the death penalty, saying, 'The dilemma of kill or be killed, which confronts civilized society daily and inexorably, is bedeviled by the jumble of panic, superstition and angry resentment we call punishment . . .'

What would prison have been like for Mary Daly? Mr Justice Kingsmill Moore described the conditions in Mountjoy prison, Dublin, in the 1940s: 'Hard labour, in the old sense, had ceased to exist . . . weaving was the task which involved most physical exertion. Food was more than adequate in quantity and of good quality. The old exercise rings, where prisoners circled in silence, were a thing of the past and exercise was taken in small casual groups . . .'

Mary's case was reviewed by the government on 3 May 1949. She served a period of penal servitude from 1948 to 1953 and then was ten years in a convent. Seamus Breathnach has explained the place of the church in the penal system at the time: 'The RC church . . . acquired a Barabas-like power of release with respect to some prison inmates . . . The church could . . . direct penal policy for the state, not just with respect to children under their control, as we appreciate more fully in the twenty-first century, but with respect to a wide range of issues, including the education and release of prisoners . . .'

Only very rarely in criminal trials has there been such doubt and uncertainty about the actual events of a case, and the fact that so many people arrived on the scene just a little too late to have any definite evidence on the series of events in the fight only served to make the trial more complex. In the end, the inescapable fact of Mary Daly's story is that in the church on the fatal day, there were no witnesses, two women were in the church, and circumstantial evidence pointed in just one direction. All those circumstances were made much worse when, in front of the jury, the savagery appeared to be all about a small sum of money. In such instances, the biographies supplied by the prosecution are easily angled towards a back-story that fits well with the case as it is told to the court.

CHAPTER 17

Three Famous Tales from the Last Years of the Rope

... at school assembly, we were asked to pray for the soul of Vivian Teed.

Andrew Hinton

The three stories in this chapter are all famous (and certainly were in their time) because they have entered the statistics of capital punishment in Britain. The first is the case of the last man hanged in Wales; the other two are dramatic stories from the last year of judicial hanging in England. These kinds of statistics have attracted a large readership, as that terrible branch of crime writing concerned with execution and punishment still attracts attention.

1. Vivian Teed

William Williams, seventy-three years of age, was postmaster at Manselton, Swansea, in 1958. The shop and home, all one, were at Fforestfach. On the morning of 16 November 1957, young Margaret John came to work at the post office and couldn't get into the premises; but she looked inside through the letter box and there she saw, to her horror, the body of Mr Williams in the hallway. When the police came, they found that the man was dead, the victim of a savage attack. His skull was fractured; he had clearly been attacked with a hammer or something similar. The assailant had not been too worried about leaving traces – there were bloody footprints around the body and a silk stocking beneath Mr Williams.

It was a time when small corner shops and sub-post offices were particularly vulnerable to attack, often with violent attack and murder following. In most parts of the country, this was happening, and local forces were having to call out Scotland Yard and work harder than usual on the study of the crime scenes. In many of these cases the murders or assaults had been committed for quite small booty. The murder in Fforestfach was in keeping with that trend – the motive being robbery. But in this case, the suspect was soon tracked down. Vivian Teed was found and sure enough there was blood all over his clothes; he had not destroyed the shoes or trousers he had worn in the attack.

Teed had gone to the post office expecting to find no one at home. He knocked, being sure that there would be no response, but to his surprise, Mr Williams came to the door. Teed had gone there to rob the place, and he soon overcame his surprise and pushed the old man back. The killer had gone to the post officer with a weapon – a hammer – and when the old man put up a fight, Teed struck him. It took several blows, and the younger man was pulled down, and soon the man beneath him was dead.

Teed told the police, 'I went and tried all the drawers to see if there was any money. I had a look round like. He was still moving and groaning. I didn't want him to see me so I switched off the light and made for the door ...' He then put the light back on, hoping, so he said, that a policeman would see it and come to help. He said that he didn't want the old man to lose too much blood. Teed told another man about what he had done – someone called Ronald Williams at Cwmbwria; he told this man that he had never meant to kill. But the murder scene had been horrific. Teed added that Williams had managed to get up again: 'He had been struggling to get up all the time but he couldn't get a footing. It was too slippery in the blood. The last thing I saw was he was up on his knees.'

Teed, clumsy as he was, had put the silk stocking over his hands so that there would be no prints; that was to matter very little, as there was so much else that would lead the police to him. The main clue was that the hammer used had been left at the scene; Teed had worked at the post office for a short time and so he was checked out. There was a hammer missing from his father's toolbox. Also, the shoeprints in the blood soon were compared to shoes owned by Teed.

He stood in Cardiff Assizes on 17 March 1958, before Mr Justice Salmon. W L Mars Jones prosecuted and F Elwyn Jones defended, and the defence argument was for diminished responsibility. The words applied to Teed were that he had been 'suffering from an abnormality of the mind' when he killed. Only the year before the trial the new Homicide Act had stated that if the notion of diminished responsibility was accepted, then the charge had to be reduced to manslaughter. The Act had this wording:

> Where a person kills or is a party to a killing of another, he shall not be convicted of murder if he was suffering from such abnormality of mind as substantially impaired his mental responsibility for his acts and omissions in doing or being a party to the killing.

The important section also had a wide definition of such a malaise: this covered 'arrested or retarded development of mind' and 'any inherent cause induced by disease or injury'. The defence had to prove such a defence convincingly to have the manslaughter charge applied. Elwyn Jones had to argue that some force drove Teed to kill, but Mars-Jones stressed the terrible fact that twenty-seven blows had been struck. It had certainly been a frenzied and relentless attack. The forensic evidence in court, mainly given by Emlyn Davies, made it clear that in the bloodbath of the hall, there was so much left there which could be traced to a number of items of clothing belonging to Teed, that the finger of guilt had only one way to point.

What could Elwyn Jones muster as support for his defence case? He had to call on every medical testimony he could scrape together. First he had a statement by the hospital officer at HMP Swansea, and luckily he had been methodical and had monitored Teed's behaviour in prison. He told the court that Teed was 'a dangerously jealous man who needs careful watching'. It was noted that he had fits of violent temper, often more apparent when he had had a prison visit from his girlfriend. The officer also recalled that at one time, Teed had told a visitor that he hit Williams because he was holding him, and that he never meant to murder him. That does not tally with the twenty-seven blows of course. Manslaughter would hardly apply there. However, perhaps, Elwyn Jones must have thought, diminished responsibility might be easier to prove given the manic actions of 'overkill' in the attack.

There was also Dr Eurfyl Jones, the consultant psychiatrist from St David's Hospital, Caernarvon. His words were not really specific enough to offer a clear perception, as he summed up Teed as 'a psychopathic personality'. At that time, a jury would have had difficulties grasping the implications of that. Yet the biography of the accused would seem to align with a familiar murderous and dangerous character: he was from a family of nine, born in Swansea, and then had been evacuated into the country in the war. He certainly had a criminal record – three previous spells inside. Dr Jones presented two opposing views: first, that Teed knew he was doing when he attacked, but that he was mentally ill. That left plenty of room for manoeuvre but then the doctor added that he did think that there was impairment of Teed's mind at the time and that the 'abnormality' was definitely apparent. But the fact remained, as he also said, that Teed had shown no remorse.

The recurrent problem of the expert witness in the matter of mental illness was a strong element in the trial. Another prison doctor, Dr Fenton, disagreed with Jones and insisted that Teed had no mental abnormality. He even stated that he did not consider Teed to be a psychopath. Elwyn Jones must have felt a shiver of defeat on hearing that opinion expressed.

The jury took almost five hours to reach a decision; they failed to reach a unanimous decision, in spite of Mr Justice Salmon directing them to think only in line with clear evidence, and to avoid supposition. One person in the jury was not convinced by the prosecution's reasoning. Salmon took control, and he said to the court: 'It is my duty to remind you that as far as impaired responsibility is concerned, it is not for the prosecution to prove that the accused had not diminished or impaired responsibility.' The Homicide Act of the previous year made it very clear as to what circumstances in a homicide made a hanging decision essential. The crucial words were about homicide committed 'in the course or furtherance of theft'.

The guilty decision was announced and Salmon told Teed that he would 'suffer death in the manner authorised by law'. The progression towards the scaffold had begun. It has to be recorded that, in a largely meaningless way, Teed was examined by psychiatrists in his death cell; the medical men were out to prove that he was not mentally ill in any way that would encourage a reprieve.

There was a petition, signed by a thousand people, and there was an appeal, with Lord Goddard presiding. The panel of appeal judges found no evidence of diminished responsibility and the appeal was dismissed. After that Teed's only chance of staying alive was an appeal to the Home Secretary for a reprieve. It did not happen, and that was announced on 25 May. He was doomed. Teed was hanged at HMP Swansea on 6 May 1958. The executioners were Robert Stewart and Harry Robinson.

That death certainly had an impact across Wales. Andrew Hinton has recorded that, with his memory of being told to pray for the soul of Vivian Teed, at his school in South Wales.

It is not often that we have accounts by judges and barristers of their formative experiences in the era of hangings, but Elwyn Jones was later to become Lord Elwyn Jones, and in his memoirs he is candid (and enlightening) about the drama and tensions in criminal trials in the early 1960s when a guilty verdict in a murder case was an appointment with the noose. As he wrote in his autobiography, 'A trial for life introduced a new dimension of drama and emotion' and he made the point, easily overlooked now, about the wording the clerk of assize used when asking for a verdict: 'Look upon the face of the prisoner and say whether he is guilty or not guilty of murder.' He also makes a great deal of the clerk's other solemn words before sentence:

> My Lords, the Queen's Justices, do strictly charge and com-
> mand all persons to Keep silence while sentence of death is
> passed upon the prisoner at the bar . . .

2. Richard Latham

The case of Richard Latham was yet another involving potential diminished responsibility. He was discharged from the RAF as a 'psychopathic personality with anti-social trends'. Back in civvy street, Latham began an affair with a married woman, Doreen Wass. They met in early 1963, and not long after she borrowed a large sum of money from Latham, but then left him and went into hiding. He searched for her, and with a feeling of revenge and hurt pride, he had violent intentions towards her.

Latham went to see Mr Wass and insisted on being told where Doreen was. When the husband refused to say, he was assaulted, and Latham, according to later testimony, at first wanted to give her 'a good hiding' but then his thoughts turned to murder. In May 1964 he bought a revolver and in November that year he found out where she was.

He went to her house, intending to use the gun, but he saw that she was pregnant so he waited until the child was born and then returned. On that second occasion, he couldn't do it and went away. But after that his dark and dangerous resolve took hold of him: he went a third time went into the house, and shot her three times at close range. He told police later that at first, going to her with the gun, he had been frightened. But when he did finally shoot, there was no doubt that her life would be taken. He went home, then hid the spent cartridges, bullets and some glasses inside a glove and put the glove in his henhouse.

But later his feeble attempts to cover himself, such as disguising himself with the glasses and then hiding the items, all disappeared into a straightforward admission of guilt to the police when they came. He simply said, 'It is all right . . . I am the man you are looking for. It was I that shot her.' Again, when asked where the gun was, he acted in the same way, at first saying he had thrown it over a railway embankment but then coming clean and telling police where it really was.

He said, 'I did think I might get away with it at first, but when it came to it I was not bothered.' That was to be the start of yet another lengthy debate on the theme of mental abnormality. But at first the outcome was clear: three doctors gave evidence – two for the defence made much of his past history, and of course he had already been labelled a psychopath. But the fact is that the medical officer of Armley jail, who had actually seen and observed the man, rather than simply applying theory from established documentation, spoke for the prosecution. The jury did not accept diminished responsibility and Latham was found guilty.

His case went to the appeal court, and there the case argued was that the evidence about Latham's mental instability was clear, and should be reconsidered in the light of the key word in the 1957 Act, 'impaired' ability to function mentally. But the evidence of the doctors was unchallenged. As the report of the appeal said at the time: 'In particular, it was put to Dr Roberts and Dr O'Brien (for the defence) that for a very long time Latham had determined to kill this woman, that from November onwards he knew where she was, and that, although he had been the subject of psychological disorder some eleven years previously . . . this was not a case of giving way to sudden impulses . . .'

The decision as to mental impairment was for the jury to decide and they had done that. Dr Wray was the expert who was most forthright in saying that he was uncertain about Latham's 'impairment.' In the Act the impairment had to be 'substantial' and the doctor could not assert that with any confidence. The official appeal report concluded:

> If there are facts which would entitle a jury to reject or differ from the opinions of the medical men, this court would not, and could not, disturb their verdict, but if the doctors' evidence is unchallenged and there is no other on this issue, a verdict contrary to their opinion would not be 'a true verdict in accordance with the evidence'.

That decision was on 28 April. A week later, after an appeal for a reprieve, it was granted by the Home Secretary. Soon after the trial, the Murder (Death Penalty) Act suspended the capital punishment for murder for a period of five years, to be made permanent if that could be agreed, after that five years.

3. David Chapman

But Latham was not the very last man to be sentenced to die in England. That distinction goes to twenty-three-year-old John Chapman, who was charged with the murder of Alfred Harland, a man of sixty-five, who was drowned while Chapman and his friend Makinson were, in the words of the 1957 Act, 'in the furtherance of theft'. The two men drowned Mr Harland in the North Bay swimming pool in Scarborough. The killers were both Scarborough men; only Chapman was found guilty of murder, as Makinson was found to be an accessory and was guilty of grievous bodily harm. The two assailants had said that Mr Harland had merely fallen into the water.

The two men had broken into the office at the pool and stolen £51-3s-7d. It was a small sum to grab by way of a killing.

Mr Harland was a nightwatchman and had tried to face the robbers. There was no doubt that the death happened while a theft was in progress.

Chapman was sentenced to death on 4 November. Five days later, capital punishment in England was suspended for five years. Finally, on 16 December 1969, the abolition was confirmed. Chapman was reprieved.

Shortly before abolition was announced, Ducan Sandys, the MP for Streatham, raised a petition asking for the re-establishment of hanging; 8,000 people living in Sussex signed it. Sandys told the press: 'We have found all over Britain that about 85 per cent of those who are approached readily sign the petition which simply asks that the death penalty should be restored for murder.'

But, opposing this, just a month before the announcement of abolition, thirty prominent criminologists wrote to *The Times* to state that '... such evidence as there is suggests that the rate of murder in society is a function of infinitely more complex and psychological factors. We believe that to return to the situation as it obtained under the Homicide Act of 1957 ... would be shot through with unjust anomalies ...'

Those 'anomalies' are clearly reflected in the murder trials in the ten preceding years. The jury decisions, the expert witnesses and the directions of judges all combine in these trial reports to remind us that the situation was actually riddled with uncertainties and contradictions. One man would walk to the scaffold while another would walk free. As for Chapman, he was in the death cell when the more welcome kind of suspension was announced. He must have whooped with joy, we might think, but in fact, records show that late reprieves tend to produce a stunned, shocked period of stupor and trauma. After all, a person moves swiftly from acceptance to giddy appreciation of unexpected freedom.

CHAPTER 18

Hull's Great
Unsolved Mystery

*This investigation is not exhausted,
but Humberside's murder rate has
soared in recent years and it is a
case of prioritising.*

DS Morriss, Humberside Police

There are few murders as upsetting and repulsive as those of children. Killing a child, and mixing that with sexual assault or rape, makes us search for words that adequately describe the response we feel. The words we use – 'heinous' or 'repellent', or even 'barbaric', fall short of the emotive pull on us as such an outrage. When such crimes happen in our homes, the sense of revulsion is even greater. In this case the killer had an hour in which to work – the guardian of the child was out for just one hour – and the lurking, calculating killer struck.

On 9 March 1984, nine-year-old Christopher Laverack was in his sister's house in East Hull; he had been taken there by his parents as it had been arranged that his sister, Kim and her husband, Stephen, would look after him. The couple had a baby, just nine months old, and that night Stephen went out to the *Crown*, where Kim worked, to buy some crisps for young Christopher. That was at a 9.15pm. When Stephen went home again an hour later, there was no Christopher. His own little son, Martin, was crying, and there was no one else in the house. The most notable change in the room was that the television was missing.

The search for him began. Then, almost two days later, a dog-walker at Beverley Beck saw a plastic sack in the water and on investigation, that parcel proved to be a roll of carpet overlay in which was the body of Christopher. He had been sexually abused and then battered to death. A mystery had begun: no knowledge of where the boy was killed was ever gained, and the murder weapon was never located either. There had been sightings – a man had come to the house in that hour when the two children were alone – and a car had been seen parked outside.

In 2004, a feature in the *Police Review* focused on DS Morriss as the cold case was looked at again. The first phase of the murder hunt was in the hands of DCS Peter Baker, and he retired with the case still unsolved. The murder remained very much in the arena of public interest and activity, though, especially after someone donated the huge sum of £100,000 for information leading to the arrest and conviction of the killer. There was even a determined effort by a local charity, SCARF, to solve the case, but it still remained a mystery.

The twenty-year anniversary of the boy's death was the ideal time to think again, and DS Morriss said then that 'attempting to bring closure to the inquiry' had 'proved a learning exper-ience for a force that previously had only limited experience of cold case investigations.' Morriss took charge of the case in 2000 and he was faced with all kinds of difficulties when he reviewed the details of the investigation, mainly that of the retirement of some of the officers originally involved. One of the original sergeants who worked on the case had died by 2004. Those officers who were asked about the case had forgotten many of the details of course. The one person you would want to talk to in such a situation would be the scene of crime officer, and Morriss commented that the officer had forgotten the process of the scene being studied.

One of the most discouraging aspects of the cold case work then was that some of the boxed physical evidence had been destroyed when Morriss started work; the obvious question to ask is what about DNA sampling? Again, even as recently as 2004, forensic work had not brought any new knowledge to light. The heart of the challenge for Morriss and colleagues was, as was said at the time, the Humberside Police had little formal process in place for cold case work.

What about the place where Christopher's body was found? We might think that a close look at that would lead to some ideas about where the killing took place. But the material environment around the Beverley Beck had changed by 2004 also. Morriss, a man born in the area, told his interviewer, John Dean, 'I am a local man, but I have difficulty recognising that stretch of the beck – so much has changed. But one thing remains: at the time Christopher's body was found, it was a stretch of beck that was not particularly well known, which leads us to think that the killer had local knowledge.'

The one potentially very useful item needed by the investigation was the missing television, and when the beck was dredged in 2003, that seemed to be a chance to find the it, but the dredging was unsuccessful. With all this discouraging list of dead-ends and frustrations, the one thing that police would still have as an asset would be the public, and there has never been any shortage of response there. Endless lines of thought have been explored, and minor observations followed up. In 2004, Morriss said, 'We get something every month ... but because the case is so emotive and everyone had their own views and theories, we have tended to keep it out of the press.' The work of appealing for information, naturally, was always strong: from the first moment available, Pam Cawley, Christopher's mother, made several appeals for help. Six years ago, Morriss summed up the situation: 'Either the killer never told anyone about committing the crime, or somebody out there has suspicions but has kept quiet because they are concerned about the implications.'

Then in May, 2008, the media were keen to tell the public that the chief suspect in the case had died in prison. What more frustrating development could there have been? DS Higgins of Humberside Police said that the man's death could lead to new witnesses coming forward.' He was right. Two months later, the identity of the dead man, who had died of cancer in jail just a few months before his due release date, was revealed: he was Melvyn Read, Christopher's uncle. Other potential offences of child sex abuse were levelled at Read, and it emerged that he was the prime suspect for the murder of Christopher. He had been questioned but released in 2006 in connection with the case.

Police told the press in 2008, 'There is a substantial amount of evidence linking Read with the murder of Christopher.' The dead man was sixty-four.

What we are left with is the staggering thought that a common view of paedophiles and killers related to that condition is that they are planners with an instinct. Time and again we read of cases in which a child has been abducted and then later killed and abused, and that crime has taken place when a 'window of opportunity' arises – a moment when the prey is attainable. There have been such cases in which a child had been abducted from its own home, taken from bed while sleeping and pulled through a window; there have been cases in which a family at a caravan site or beach have been located, watched and then deprived of a child. Such killers are akin to animals, hunters, waiting and watching for the time to strike and for their hunger to be appeased.

This makes far more sense than some of the theories put forward. There have even been writers who have insisted that there are cults indulging in human sacrifice around and that Christopher was a victim of such a cult. Surely the more generalised but credible line of thought about a relative or person who knew him well is the one that counts. After all, a boy would open the door to a relative, and that would be seen as a normal event, although observers who noticed the car outside did not appear to say that the same car had been seen before. The explanations about the most likely events of that night are where the attention must lie: not in the fanciful and desperate imaginings on which our moral panics thrive.

The Laverack case has to be defined in just those three resonant but somehow inadequate words. The fact is that a small boy suffered a terrible death and the most likely killer has evaded justice by dying: so we have that infinite silence, something just as empty and tormenting as the thought of this being a story with no possibility of closure. There may be other lines of thought still to come, but we have to say that these are likely to be as tantalising and ultimately frustrating as some of the theories in the earlier phases of investigation.

CHAPTER 19

Sentenced to Die:
Two Manx Cases

*I do not now believe that any one of
the hundreds of executions I carried
out has in any way acted as a
deterrent against future murder...*

Albert Pierrepoint

In 1079, Godfred Crovan invaded the Isle of Man and in his reign the Tynwald parliament was established; and still today, on Tynwald Hill, the impressive seat of government stands proud. Her Majesty the Queen is now Lord of Man, and she was there in 1979 when the millennium celebrations took place at Tynwald. This might suggest a place out of step or antiquated when we come to matters of law, but in fact the truth is that Man has simply had different legal traditions and processes. The Tynwald was not really reformed until 1866, and at that time the first island police force was established, with a Chief Constable based in Douglas.

But when it comes to criminal law, they were still sentencing people to death there as recently as 1992, when Deemster Callow sentenced Anthony Teare to die for capital murder. Teare's story, with that of arguably the most troublesome and problematic Manx murder case in its history back in 1872, provides the sensational stories for this chapter.

First the High Court of Man has to be explained and an account of what existed before it was created. It was formed in 1884. From then on serious crimes have been heard at the Court of General Gaol Delivery. A judge called the Second Deemster presides, and the Court handles every trial by a court of summary jurisdiction. The jury is of seven, not twelve, people. Traditionally, there have been two Deemsters, and courts were always held in the main towns. Since 1921 there has been a court of criminal appeal, so today there is a vague comparison between English crown courts and the Man Court of General Gaol Delivery.

But in 1872 the disparities came into public notice with the case of John Kewish. He committed murder at a time when the Isle of Man's various methods of execution were simplified into hanging only: previously, before 1817, there had been several possibilities: traitors, regardless of sex, were hanged, drawn and quartered, but male felons were hung, and female felons sewn into a sack and thrown into the sea.

Kewish lived with his old parents and a disabled sister. In a family argument, he killed his father with a pitchfork. The setting was the isolated family farm at Sulby Glen. The High Bailiff of Ramsey was told of the affair, and fortunately he acted quickly, because the family were about to carry on with the funeral arrangements as if this was just another natural death. It was far from that. The source of the confrontation went back to a law suit from the father against the son for £42. That debt had supposedly been settled when John gave his father a cow.

The constable who arrived first said in court that he had heard Kewish say, in Manx, to his mother: 'Be careful and say just what you need to say, on oath . . . We'll get to the end of this day and it will be well.' The constable also said that Kewish had told him that his father had deserved such a fate for a long time, as he had been stealing sheep, and he had also been 'thrashing' Mrs Kewish for as long as John could recall.

The surgeon was F S Tellett, and he described the injuries and cause of death: 'We observed two wounds on the right side of his chest . . . Both of these were puncture wounds and on passing a probe into one, it penetrated about eight inches.' The surgeon and his assistants also found four more wounds on the back, and they noted that the lungs were collapsed and clotted blood in the airway. Death had been caused by a deep cut across the aorta.

Mrs Kewish was noted as saying that Johnny would 'have more life now' that the father was gone. That was indeed full or irony as the death sentence was to be passed. There were no other suspects, and the pitchfork had been used to kill Mr Kewish. John was the only man with a motive, and the main complication was whether or not Kewish was simple-minded.

The jury went to consider the evidence and it took fourteen hours. Even then no verdict was reached. A new trial with a new jury followed.

The obvious next move was for the defence counsel to argue for a defence of insanity. They reasoned that his mental defectiveness was enough to free him from a murder charge. But this failed, and the second jury found him guilty. He was sentenced to death by the Deemster, Mr Drinkwater. The *Isle of Man Times and Advertiser* reported this with a maximum dramatic effect:

> The names of the jurors having been called over by the Clerk of the Rolls, the Deemster asked the usual question: 'Gentlemen, are you agreed on your verdict?
>
> Mr BACKWELL (for the jury): 'Yes, your Honour.'
>
> DEEMSTER: 'Do you find the prisoner guilty or not guilty?
>
> Mr BACKWELL, 'Guilty your Honour.'
>
> The Deemster addressed the prisoner at the Bar: 'I do not know whether you have manifested any remorse for having committed so dreadful a crime. What have you to say why sentence should not be passed upon you for the crime you have committed?'
>
> The prisoner made no reply . . .

The words and the ritual had been said so many times. The sentence of death was then passed. He was sent back to prison at Castle Rushen to await his execution. But there was hope of a reprieve: the Queen could have reduced this to life imprisonment, but the Home Office took over that responsibility. Efforts were made, with the Lieutenant-Governor gathering statements which would appeal for leniency in the case. It turned out that in the first trial, five of the jurors had told the authorities that the majority were for an acquittal. The information about Mr Kewish's violence towards his wife was a factor, no doubt. But the Home Office took no notice of anything the Lieutenant-Governor submitted and the Queen was told by the Home Secretary that mercy could not be condoned.

The fact was that the Queen was not comfortable with the apparent duty of her being involved, and she wrote to the

Home Secretary making clear her unease and displeasure at this responsibility. Once more, the clash of Manx law with that of English law was apparent, and it was determined that this would be put right in case there were other capital offences comitted on the island which would make this situation arise again. There had been no execution on the island for half a century, and there were practical obstacles in that it proved to be hard to have a gallows erected.

Eventually the national hangman, William Calcraft, came over to carry out the dictates of the law. As the old hangman was busy, handling judicial killings from London to Scotland and now on the Isle of man, Wiliam Marwood in Lincoln was developing the more humane calculation of the 'long drop' *Reynolds News* reported the scene on 11 August. It had been a private execution, but with the press present. The reporter noted that Calcraft had arrived by boat from Liverpool and was recognised. A mob walked with him for some way until he took a cart to Castletown.

Not long before the date of execution, Kewish made a confession to PC Thomas Kneale:

> My father was ready to go to bed, with his jacket and waistcoat off, and sitting by the fire on a stool, smoking, when the Devil tempted me to shoot him. I came out of my own room and struck my father in the back. The gun was charged with four slugs. I fired the gun and my father fell, saying '*Chee Chreese*' which means 'the peace of Christ go with you' . . .

Kewish also said that Satan made him do and that it was because he 'had no schooling and 'knew no better.' His statements demolished the forensic thinking, because he told a turnkey that the father had not been stabbed at all, but shot, confirming the story he first told the constable. His story was confirmed when a search was made for a slug in the wall of the house, where he had said it went in, and the slug was found.

Naturally, the hanging was a major event on Man after so many years without a death sentence being carried out. Mr Kermode, the prison governor, told the press that selected reporters would be allowed into the place of execution, and the writer for the *Mona Herald* told his readers exactly what he saw:

> We were conducted to the debtors' yard where we found a large and imposing structure of timber erected as a scaffold. The work had been done on a design concocted by the officers of the gaol and the builders ... it met with the entire approbation of Calcraft, who professed himself pleased with everything connected with it ... The structure is composed of a series of wooden pillars 12 feet high on which rests a smooth and firm platform around which runs a 3-foot high protection railing, which is draped in black cloth.

He then saw Calcraft arrive with his instruments of death. Kewish walked out to meet his death, the reporter noted, 'With a tread as firm as a rock'. He walked to the beam and stood, ready for the end; Calcraft put on the white hood, adjusted the rope and within a minute, Kewish was 'launched into eternity'. Readers of the *Mona Herald* absorbed the fact that 'Death was instantaneous. Not a movement of the shoulders, scarcely a vibration of a limb, testified to the quick and certain fatality of the law's revenge.' The most nervous man there had been the chaplain, who just managed to say, while trembling, 'Lord, receive the soul of John Kewish.'

The very last death sentence passed in the United Kingdom was on Anthony Teare, on the Isle of Man, so once again, that island takes centre stage in criminal history. Teare was described as a 'loner with low self-esteem' who murdered a young woman, possibly as a contract killing, but that is not certain. He was found guilty of murder in 1992, and sentenced to death. Amazingly, no commutation of the sentence immediately followed, as was the usual practice. But an appeal followed, and the conviction was found to be unsafe. Everything about the case was singular: he was not acquitted, but a retrial was to take place; yet before that new trial could be arranged, something radical happened to the constitution and the criminal code, revising the code of 1872: the death penalty was abolished and life imprisonment for murder was put in its place.

Still, Teare was retried: he was found guilty of murder in 1994 and he was sentenced to life imprisonment. The Isle of Man may not have often figured in British criminal history, but these two murder cases certainly caused a stir, and they provide astonishing statistics whenever questions of capital punishment occur. The tales of Kewish and Teare provide stories in which the consequences of the crimes impact on the central criminal justice system in England. Although the legal traditions of the Isle of Man have been very different from those in England, the anomalous procedures and protocol of the island have given the lawyers considerable headaches, and of course, have also given Queen Victoria a notable crisis of conscience and given cause for concern from the 'Widow of Windsor' who preferred to keep well clear of the criminal law and its responsibilities.

CHAPTER 20

His Ghost Walks the Corridors

Prisoner at the Bar, you have been arraigned upon a charge of murder and have placed yourself upon your country. That country has now found you guilty ...

Clerk of the Assize, Nodder trial

his is the story of a lorry-driver lodger – from Hell. It is disgusting for a crime writer to see the man's name dignified with a place in the reference works of murder now established in reference libraries. But the tale has to be told.

Missing from her home ... at 11, Thoresby Avenue, Newark, since Tuesday, 5 January, 1937, Mona Lilian Tinsley, aged 10 years (rather short for age), dark hair (bobbed with fringe) rosy cheeks, four prominent teeth at the front ... It has been established that this girl was seen at Hayton Smeath, near Retford at about mid-day on Wednesday, 6 January, 1937.

(Text from a police poster)

Frederick Nodder moved into new lodgings in Newark in 1935, where his landlady was Mrs Tinsley. He didn't stay long, but he made a mark with the children. To them he was 'Uncle Fred'. He was clearly a man who was difficult to live with, at least in the adult world. When he moved on to East Retford, he still proved to be a handful for the landlady, with his bad habits and tendency to create a mess. Nodder appears to be a man with a mission – to destroy everything and everyone around him that could be classified as weak or vulnerable.

But back in Newark, the large family of Tinsleys was now one short of the usual number. Little Mona, aged ten, was missing. Her father, Wilfred, was frantic with worry. Mona did not return home from her school on the 5 January 1937. The search began. Her school was not far away and he began his search there. Mona's poor father was distraught with anxiety. After the police were called, the description went out: she was wearing a knitted suit and wore Wellingtons. But a boy called Willie Placket recalled seeing Mona talking to a man and said that he would recognise the man if he saw him again. A Mrs Hird had also seen Mona with a man 'who was a lodger with the girl's mother . . .' The net was closing in on the person described as 'a man with staring eyes'.

Nodder had a hook nose and his moustache was ginger; he seems to have been memorable, as lots of people remembered him on that journey with little Mona. A bus conductor recalled him. The police traced him to Retford and he was picked up. He had been living as Hudson, and was the father of a child living locally.

Mona had been seen with 'Uncle Fred' and consequently, as Mona was now officially missing and the anxiety increased, Nodder was interviewed. His story was that he had given the girl a lift to Sheffield, and then put Mona on a bus to her aunt's in Worksop. It was all highly suspicious and he was arrested for abduction. There was no body, so there was no murder charge. In court, the abduction still stood and he was sent to prison. As he was in custody and there was a feeling that Mona had been attacked or even killed, a massive search began; 1,000 people joined in to search areas between Retford and Newark. It was such a wide stretch of land that the police from Nottingham-shire, Lincolnshire and Derbyshire all spent time and man-power on the case.

Scotland Yard now sent men to step up the campaign. The Chesterfield canal was dragged. Nodder had been tried at Birmingham, but now off he went to Nottingham to face a murder charge.

So began Fred Nodder's period inside the walls of Lincoln prison. Only three months after his trial, Mona's body was found in the River Idle close to Bawtry. She had been strangled. Nodder was in court again, trying to tell tales to escape the noose. Nothing he could say did him any good. The presiding judge, Mr Justice Macnaughton, said, 'Justice has slowly, but surely, overtaken you and it only remains for me to pronounce the sentence which the law and justice require . . .'

The great barrister, Norman Birkett, had spoken for the prosecution; it was to be his last trial, appearing for the Crown. It was a terrible case, with a widespread sense of outrage around it, as Nodder had sexually assaulted Mona before killing her. 'Uncle Fred' had turned out to be a monster. The photos of him show a man with a matching flat cap and scarf of small check pattern and a thick overcoat. His eyes are piercing and he shows a face to the world that expresses nothing substantial. 'Something is missing in him' as is often said of these types of killers. Here was a twisted personality who enjoyed inflicting pain on helpless children. It had taken Mona five minutes to die. Ironically, this man who had created so much pain and torment to others, lived in a place called 'Peacehaven'.

He was sentenced to hang. A few days after Christmas 1937, he was in the hands of the hangman and left this world. Or did he? He was hanged in Lincoln Prison on Greetwell Road, and his last moments would have been on the wing of the execution suite. He would have fallen through the trap to dangle and die – very quickly – taking less time to expire than his victim had done. The corpse was taken down and buried, with quicklime, as was the custom. But was that the last of Fred Nodder inside the prison walls? Some think not.

Since then, there has been development in the prison, as there has with almost every other Victorian building. Staff report sightings of a man walking the corridors, a man with a dark overcoat and flat check cap. One report is of turning a corner to see a man with piercing eyes coming towards you. Some have merely glimpsed the profile, with the hooked nose and moustache.

There are many dark roads and corners around Greetwell Road. A spirit could wander those streets, a restless, evil entity like Uncle Fred. If the tales are true, then this evil man is as restless now as he was in life – always open to do some horrible mischief. In fairly recent times, when building work was done on the prison site, the graves of executed prisoners were taken up and carried to the city cemetery. The more serious ghost hunters date the appearances of the ghost of Uncle Fred to that time. When the ground opened up, his nasty spirit walked into the world again, out to disturb the unwary. The man with the staring eyes, if he exists in spirit form, will still try his hardest to unsettle the unwary night-walker. Nodder was always a man who haunted, loitered, and watched people.

Even if the Lincoln walker through Greetwell Road has no belief in ghosts, a glance at the forbidding high and dark walls of the prison there will do enough to suggest that this killer had no pleasant stay in his last hours on earth.

CHAPTER 21

Miscarriage of Justice – by Earprint

Elected silence, sing to me, and beat upon my whorled ear.

G M Hopkins

This is one of the saddest murder stories ever told. The reason for that sadness is that the victim was a remarkable woman who had been a wonderful servant to her community: humanitarian, selfless and admirable in every way. Yet her life was ended at the hands of a heartless killer, unknown to this day. But this sad story also has a parallel – a tale of offbeat and wonderful forensics.

On 7 May 1996, Dorothy Wood, aged ninety-four and weighing only 6 stones, was found dead in her bed at her home in Whitby Avenue, Fartown, Huddersfield. She had been smothered, and it was clear that her home had been burgled; the attacker had taken her life in the course of robbing her. Her neighbours told the press later that, as Dorothy was deaf, they had to write everything down for her as she was unable to lip-read. It was a horrendous, callous killing. A reward of £5,000 was offered for information leading to an arrest and conviction.

It didn't take long to arrest a suspect – the evidence of an earprint on one of the house's windows led police to Mark Dallagher. A Dutch forensic expert on earprints, Cornelius van der Lugt, testified that the earprint on the window matched the ear of Dallagher: it was as convincing as a fingerprint source in its forensic value. But the defence counsel never called their own earprint expert, and Dallagher was convicted of murder.

Then, in January 2004, Dallagher was freed at an appeal hearing, the victim of a serious miscarriage of justice. A retrial was ordered in 2002 as his conviction was unsafe then; a new investigation was set in motion, and further forensic study began. DNA played a part in that new work, and it was announced that, as the press report said: 'West Yorkshire police and the Crown Prosecution Service later issued a statement about the case, which was originally heard at Leeds Crown Court. They said that when the Court of Appeal ordered a retrial, "it made no criticism of the way in which the Crown had presented its case at the first trial."'

The case had made legal history as it was the first trial in which ear prints led to a successful prosecution. There is a terrible irony in the statement made at the time by one lawyer that such forensics was 'a great leap forward for forensic science'. What had been done to make it certain that Dallagher was innocent?

The basis for study is that the human ear, when pressed to a flat surface, forms a two-dimensional print; each one of such prints is reckoned to be unique – an anatomical pointer to the person. Collection of a copy of the print is similar to the methods used in taking copies of finger prints. But there is now no absolute certainty on this and the jury is out on the nature of expert evidence. The National Training Centre for Scientific Support to Crime Investigation is establishing a database based on further research. It follows that, in a court of law, one expert will be against another, as in all areas of forensic evidence in earlier years of crime investigation. There is always a period of uncertainty in any area of forensic expertise; even DNA sampling had a 'teething period' for both the science itself and for the application of knowledge to court procedure.

Just a year before Dallagher's conviction, a conference for shoeprint and toolmark examiners was held in Holland, and in a paper given there on ear prints by Mr van der Lugt, he states that an earlier researcher had said that 'The ear has the most characteristic feature elements of the human body thanks to the variation in height and depth of the form. It has such a great quantity of different forms that that it is almost impossible to find two persons with parts that are absolutely identical. Besides that the form of the ear does not change from birth to death.' That seems like a very strong basis of thought for the man who stood there at Leeds Crown Court and said that Dallagher's ear was easily linked to the earprint.

There was also some reassurance for the CPS and police in the examples from earlier investigations, such as one from 1985 in which a raid on a banker and his wife near Rotterdam left some evidence for detectives – the print of a left and right ear on a door – and this led to the arrest of the attacker. Van der Lugt wrote: 'Now the ear prints are the only traces that can lead to the identity of the offender.'

But then, as Dallagher, an innocent man, was stuck in a prison cell, DNA analysis was more refined than in the earlier days in the mid-1980s and along came methods by which less substantial residual material could be tested for DNA sequences. The earprint in taken Fartown was not that of Mr Dallagher.

In fact, there is doubt about the use of earprint forensics. Before Dallagher was freed, Professor Peter van Coppen, of Leiden University, stated that there were limitations in the research: 'There has been no research done in which you can say, for instance, what the national distribution of lobes is, so you don't know if the ear print is one which would match 80% of everyone else's or whether it has unique characteristic.' Van der Lugt, apparently, does not agree. That difference in expert opinion, it is clear, can open the floodgates to other appeals for potential miscarriages of justice from ear print evidence, as in the case of Albert James, for instance, who was convicted on earprint evidence at Preston Crown Court – he was convicted on earprint evidence when no fingerprints were found. Earprints as a second-best print source of evidence are clearly under a shadow of doubt now.

Dorothy Wood, as her biographer Graham Thurgood has written, was born in 1901 and trained as a nurse in Halifax, gaining qualification as a midwife also and spent four years working as a Queen's Nurse. She later went to Canada on a scholarship and then returned to work in Yorkshire. Graham Thurgood sums up her achievement: 'All who have watched her career have been impressed by her enthusiasm for her work. She has had remarkable success in all her examinations ... and excellent reports form those in authority.' She retired in 1956, after doing a stint of health visiting. In other words, she had made a massive contribution to the health and well-being to thousands of people in the Huddersfield area, and the end of her life, killed by an intruder, was indeed a terrible injustice and somehow tragic in the most dignified sense of the word. There must have been a certain level of satisfaction when an arrest and conviction followed. But her real killer remains unknown.

Whoever broke into her home that night found her in bed on the ground floor, as she had a heart condition, and it is surely the case that the intruder saw a danger of the alarm being raised and took the easiest action possible. He would have thought that such a manner of death might be taken as something happening through natural causes, as Dorothy was so old and frail. It all has a nasty ring of truth about it – a simple theory of the narrative of the murder that night in Fartown.

A memorial service was held at Woodhouse Parish Church in 1996 and there was a memorial bench placed near her home in Fartown. Her good deeds and public service record will live on in the minds of those who knew her.

As for Mark Dallagher, he spent almost seven years in gaol for a crime he did not commit. He had always said he was innocent, and had even made it clear to police at the time that he was ill with an ankle injury and could not have done a burglary. He spoke to the press and said, 'I've waited seven years for this day. I've spent six of those years in prison, pro-testing my innocence to deaf ears. The last nine months has been a terrible ordeal all as a result on the prosecution's reliance on now discredited expert evidence.'

The science will go on though. At the moment, there are efforts to streamline ear print evidence by using computerised data. In a paper written for the journal, *Legal Medicine*, G N Rutty and others suggest that it is possible to use a computer-ised ear print identification system. They add: 'To assist those considering similar developments we share the concept and possible solutions we have identified and encountered to date, and highlight the advantages for such a system over traditional manual methods used for ear print identification.' In other words, we are still at the 'back to the drawing board' stage in this context.

It is amazing to think that the use of earprints is not new. They were being studied as evidence in investigations back in Victorian times. Surely we have to pity the poor villains who were caught by these very questionable means. So the jury is out

– but unfortunately for Mr Dallagher, his jury were 'in' – and were convinced by the science they were asked to understand. Today, it is easy to imagine one expert pitched against another, even though data may be computerised – in the middle would be the baffled jury of laypeople, trying to grasp the identifying markers of specific ear prints and coping with the technical jargon involved.

The murder of Dorothy Wood remains a mystery, and so does the value of the earprint as forensic evidence.

Epilogue

T he murder cases here have proved to be as varied, enigmatic and unpredictable as murder itself. It is an offence against both morality and socially-constructed law that goes back to Cain and Abel. Yet its fascination goes on. My own contact with murderers has involved meeting those who kill for cash, some who kill for revenge, and many others who have taken a life or lives because or irresistible urges. Much crime is opportunist and a great deal is to do with patience and forebearance ebbing away after years of emotional attrition. Yet still the majority of killers know their victims; still the majority of killings happen within the doors of apparently blissful domesticity. Time and again we hear people talk about the 'nice couple' at No 21, and those statements are made after the nice husband has killed his nice wife. What strikes the observer in the major cases is the mixed nature of the investigation processes: 'uneven' would be the polite adjective to use. The back-up from forensics has been a very slow and piecemeal business as well, yet what becomes obvious in the last few decades is the clash between new advances in forensics and the use of expert evidence in court. Even with the refinement of DNA sampling techniques, there have still been the logistic problems of making scientific method understandable to the jury. Some of the more recent murder trials may have lacked the exuberance and dramatic skill of some of the great barristers of the past, but often they make up for that lack by their sheer bizarre or complex nature. Of course, the coda to many famous murders from the past, or even the recent past, is the story of the offender after the life sentence. But as prison memoirs become more easily available and the need for documentaries to be disseminated across the mass media increases, prison becomes more open and comprehensible. Yet in spite of this, we all know, as Oscar Wilde expressed it:

All that we know who lie in gaol
Is that the wall is strong;

And that each day is like a year,
A year whose days are long.

My point is that the accepted murder story is never really complete – at least, not since the end of hanging in Britain at least. The convict enters a personal suspension of time, a limbo, as Wilde understood.

On the other side of the story, the tale of the detectives, lawyers and victims, material is more sketchy and elusive. But in the end, a murder story will still draw attention and sell magazines, newspapers and films. The run of the mill taking of a life will still be compelling. George Orwell, in his essay, *Decline of the English Murder* (1946), describes a typical English Sunday afternoon, one in which father had eaten and then fills a pipe and wants something to read: Orwell writes: 'In these blissful circumstances, what is it that you want to read about? Naturally, about a murder ...' That had been the case since ballads were first sung, about *Tom Dooley* or about *The Night before Larry was Stretched*.

Acknowledgements

Thanks go to my editor, Brian Elliott, to Vicki Schofield who produced some excellent line drawings, and to the archivists and librarians from the East Riding Archives, Hull History Centre, National Archives of Ireland and Lincolnshire Archives. For general advice and good conversation on some outstanding cases, I am grateful to Richard Whittington-Egan, the doyen of true crime writing today.

Bibliography and Sources

So many of the sources for many of these murder cases are in obscure places; yet some have been written about until there is surely nothing less to say. Despite changing tastes in crime history and true crime writing, some writers abide as classics, masters of the genre. Outstanding among these are William Roughead, Colin Wilson and Richard Whittington-Egan. The references here to their books, while merely in an alphabetical list, deserve a special mention. Roughead's account of the Jeannie Donald murder is, in many aspects, a masterly template for case-book writing.

Other sources have been official, and the HMSO publications of inquiries have to be some of the very best materials for this genre. Without the perspective of inquiries, much of the drama of reprieves, pardons and the search for the dark truths of murder would work only on one limited level.

Books
Abbott, Geoffrey, *Execution* (Summersdale, 2005).
Airne, C W, *The Story of the Isle of Man* (Norris Modern Press, 1964).
Beadle, Jeremy and Harrison, Ian, *Firsts, Lasts and Onlys: Crime* (Robson Books, 2007).
Beaven, Colin, *Fingerprints* (Fourth Estate, 2003).
Browne, D G and Tullett, E V, *Bernard Spilsbury: His Life and Cases* (Companion Book Club, 1952).
Camps, F E with Barber, R, *The Investigation of Murder* (Michael Joseph, 1966).
Cecil, Henry, *The Trial of Walter Rowland* (David and Charles, 1975).
Cherrill, Fred, *Cherrill of the Yard* (Popular Book Club, 1948).
Court of Criminal Appeal Records (Sweet and Maxwell, 1946).
D'Cruze, Shani et al, *Murder* (Willan Publishing, 2006).
Denning, Lord, *Landmarks in the Law* (Butterworths, 1984).
Dernley, Syd and Newman, David, *The Hangman's Tale* (Robert Hale, 1989).
Doughty, Jack, *The Rochdale Hangman and his Victims* (Jade, 1998).
Eddleston, John J, *The Encyclopaedia of Executions* (Blake, 2000).
Eddy, J P, *Scarlet and Ermine* (William Kimber, 1960).
Ellis, John, *Diary of a Hangman* (Forum Press, 1997).
Ensor, David, *I Was a Public Prosecutor* (Robert Hale, 1958).
Fielding, Steve, *Pierrepoint: A Family of Executioners* (Blake, 2006).
Gaute, J H H and Odell, Robin, *The Murderers' Who's Who* (Pan, 1983).

Glazebrook, P R, *Blackstone's Statutes on Criminal Law 2009–2010* (OUP, 2010).

Hale, Leslie, *Hanged in Error* (Penguin, 1961).

Hodge, Harry (ed), *Famous Trials 2* (Penguin Books, 1948).

Honeycombe, Gordon, *The Murders of the Black Museum 1870–1970* (Arrow, 1984).

Humphries, Sir Travers, *A Book of Trials: personal recollections of an eminent judge of the High Court* (Pan, 1953).

Jackson, Robert, *The Chief: the biography of Gordon Hewart* (Harrap, 1959).

Jones, Lord Elwyn, *In My Time* (Weidenfeld and Nicolson, 1983).

Kadri, Sadakat, *The Trial* (Harper, 2006).

Koestler, A and Rolph, C H, *Hanged by the Neck* (Penguin, 1961).

Lane, Brian, *The Encyclopaedia of Forensic Science* (Headline, 1992).

Morrison, A C L and Hughes, E, *The Criminal Justice Act 1948* (Butterworth, 1949).

Orwell, George, *Decline of the English Murder and other Essays* (Penguin, 1953).

Report of the Royal Commission on Police Powers and Procedure (HMSO, 1929).

Roughead, William, *Tales of the Criminous* (Cassell, 1956).

Rowe, John G, *The Scaffold and the Dock* (Mellifont, 1938).

Scott, Sir Harold, *The Concise Encyclopaedia of Crime and Criminals* (Andre Deutsch, 1961).

Thomas, Donald, *Villain's Paradise* (John Murray, 2005).

Tullett, Tom, *Famous Cases of Scotland Yard's Murder Squad* (Grafton, 1988).

Vronsky, Peter, *Serial Killers: the method and madness of monsters* (Berkley Books, 2004).

Watson, Katherine, *Poisoned Lives* (Hambledon, 2003).

White, P C, *Crime Scene to Court* (Royal Society of Chemistry, 2008).

Whittington-Egan, Richard, *Speaking Volumes* (Cappella Archive, 2004).

Wilson, Colin and Seaman, Donald, *The Serial Killers* (Virgin, 2007).

Wilson, David, *Serial Killers: hunting Britons and their victims 1960–2006* (Waterside Press, 2007).

Wingate, Peter, *The Penguin Medical Dictionary* (Penguin, 1972).

Articles

Anon, 'The Aberdeen Sack Murder', *Master Detective*, January 1992, pp 2–11.

Bell, Chief Inspector A, 'The Bryant Poisoning Case', *Police Journal*, January 1938, pp 30–44.

Breathnach, Seamus, *Petty Traitors: a Short History of Capital Punishment in Ireland*, available in part at www.irishcriminology.com.

Carter, Helen, 'Murder Confession?', *Guardian.co.uk/ukcrime* 2007.

Casciani, Dominic, 'When the Murder Trail Goes Cold', *BBC News Magazine*, 6 May 2010.

Dean, John, 'Detective's Casebook – Cold Cases', *Police Review*, March 2004, pp 22–3.

Eddy, J P, 'The Infallibility of Finger-Prints', *Criminal Law Review*, 1955, pp 34–7.

Edwards, Richard, 'Will we ever get inside the Criminal Mind?', *Daily Telegraph*, 19 December, 2008).

Gibson, Barry, 'Pardon for Hanged Man Alfred Moore moves Closer', *Huddersfield Examiner*, 16 January 2010.

McGannan, Danny, 'Coming of Age', *Police Review*, May 2004, pp 22–3.

Martis, Royston, 'Never Forget', *Police Review*, October 2004, pp 18–19.

Molony, Sir Thomas, 'Prison Life in Eire and the English Criminal Justice Act', (Irish Law Society), 9 February 1949.

Moss, A W, 'Will the Moira Anderson Mystery now be Solved?', *Master Detective*, August 2003, pp 14–18.

Robinson, Andrew, 'The Murdered Policeman, the Hanged Father and a Mysterythat Lingers on', *Yorkshire Post*, 23 May 2010.

Rutty, G N, Abbas, A and Crossling, D, 'Could Earprint Identification be Computerised?', *Legal Medicine*, Vol 119, No 6, November 2005 (online).

Shaw, George Bernard, 'Capital Punishment', *The Atlantic Monthly*, 1948.

Websites

www.irishcriminolgy.com

www.cps.gov.uk

www.forensic.gov.uk/forensic

www.guardian.co.uk

www.iomguide.com/right-photos

www.springerlink.com

www.telegraph.co.uk/news

Index